Small Houses

SMALL HOUSES
Edition 2007

Author: Carles Broto
Publisher: Carles Broto
Editorial Coordinator: Jacobo Krauel
Graphic designer & production: Pilar Chueca, Carol Ferreira
Text: contributed by the architects, edited and translated by William George, Marta Rojals

© Carles Broto i Comerma
Jonqueres, 10, 1-5, Barcelona 08003, Spain
Tel.: +34 93 301 21 99
Fax: +34-93-301 00 21
info@linksbooks.net
www. linksbooks.net

All rights reserved. No part of this book may be used or reproduced in any manner whatsoever without written permission except in the case of brief quotations embodied in critical articles and reviews.

Small Houses

index

8	Schmidt, Hammer & Lassen / Bjarne Hammer A resort for holiday
18	The weeHouse team / Warner + Asmus weeHouse
30	Rojkind arquitectos PR House 34
40	Rafael Iglesia House on the Riverside"
48	Atelier Bow - Wow Asama House
58	Takaharu + Yui Tezuka / Tezuka Architects, Masahiro Ikeda / mias Engawa House
66	Bellemo & Cat Cocoon House
78	Denton & Corker & Marshall Marshall House
86	Peter Hulting Architect / Meter Arkitektur Guest Appearance
96	Takaharu+Yui Tezuka / Tezuka Architects, Masahiro Ikeda / Masahiro Ikeda co.,ltd Roof House
110	Tadao Ando 4 x 4 House

122	Crosson Clarke Carnachan Architects
	Coromandel Bach

132	KHR AS Arkitekter
	Guesthouse at Nissum Bredning

144	mae architects
	m-House

150	Alberto Campo Baeza
	De Blas House

160	Arkkitehtisuunnittelu Huttunen & Lipasti
	Villa Linnanmäki

172	Koh Kitayama + architecture workshop
	TN House

184	KOZ Architectes (Plan 01)
	House in Soulac-sur-Mer

194	Takao Shiotsuka
	Shigemi House

204	Jarmund/Vigsnæs
	Villa Flindt

214	Hertl.Architekten
	Steinwendtner House

226	Strindberg Arkitekter AB
	Villa Näckros

introduction

Great architectural works are not necessarily those that are measured by the number of square meters. Creation depends on the space and the possibilities that it affords. Therefore, architectural work in small spaces is often a challenge in which one must achieve the seemingly impossible: to turn a small space into a comfortable dwelling in which the lack of living space is not perceived.

The aim of this book is to show those designs that stand out for their skill in creating stimulating environments in small spaces. This is a complicated task that is not limited to removing partitions, building mezzanines and incorporating specific furniture for the needs of the space. A skillful use of a small space requires far more: one must also think of the requirements and the comfort of the clients, and devise an aesthetic design in which the architecture can adapt to the restrictions of a limited floor area. A total of 22 works show the imaginative force of the designs in which small premises can be transformed into comfortable dwellings, regardless of their original use or location.

The designs include apartments created after the division of a large flat, small single-family dwellings in the country and terraced fantasy dwellings. They are complemented by plans and explanations of the architectural work carried out in each scheme, all of which is proof positive that creative design does not depend on the available floor space

Schmidt, Hammer & Lassen / Bjarne Hammer

A resort for holiday

This holiday home is sited at Juelsminde in Jutland, ensconced in a wooded area at the tip of a promontory, just minutes' walking distance from north- and south-facing beaches. When the family bought the land the only structures on it were a couple of shacks, so modest in size that, tucked up in their bunk beds at night, they could tell each other stories while the wind whistled through the treetops. The experience of those shared days of living together in a small chalet set amid the pristinity of nature sparked the idea of a new cottage that would replace the old.

The cottage comprises two rectangular volumes (904 sqft): a larger communal dwelling complemented by an annex that virtually abuts it. Both volumes are designed as frames that allow light and space to stream through the open and extensively glazed long sides - timber casings of the cottage's functions and of the vistas that present themselves to the viewer looking through the house.

Beneath the roof and spanning its twin gables, the larger structure features the cottage's expansive high-ceilinged living space: a freestanding kitchen, a dining- and living area plus patio.

The larger building's two long sides face southwest and northwest, respectively, and are basically wide open to the landscape. To the southwest, eleven identical perpendicular panels of glass span ceiling and floor, yielding a transparent façade that opens up with ease. The cottage's occupants thus enjoy the amenity of being able to step straight out onto the patio along the entire length of the living area. The kitchen, a rectangular concrete unit, extends from the body of the cottage out onto the patio - accentuating the fact that here indoor activities blend into outdoor ones.

On the opposite side of the communal living space, the smaller unit is punched into the larger building's northwest-facing glass façade. Set against the extensive glazing of the cottage proper, the annex presents itself as a detached and independent volume. Moreover, the annex delivers the cottage's functional axis, as defined by compactly integrated spaces: three alcove-style bedrooms featuring twin bunk beds with immediate and open access to the main building, and separated from the natural environment only by glazing, a feature that also marks the bathroom/toilet facilities, and cupboard niches. A quartet of small gates means that the children can step outside from each of the three alcoves as well as from the bathroom area.

The annex has a floor level one step up from the main building - a slight counterpoint to what is otherwise an immediate transition from the capaciousness of the main building to the sleeping quarters of the smaller.

Location:
Juelsminde, Jutland, Denmark
Photographs:
Larsenform.com

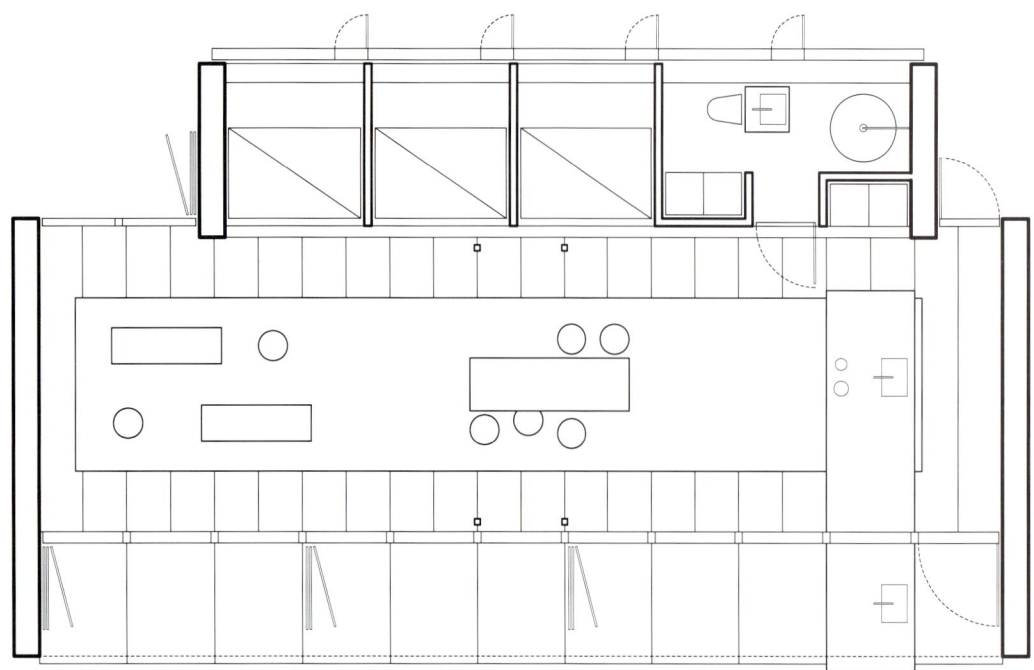

On every dimension, to minimize as far as possible the disjunction between inside and out, and thereby achieve a pervasive simplicity. To reduce the total square meters within and thereby gain an infinitely greater world outside. To keep the furnishings spare and thereby sharpen our awareness of each other, the flow of conversation, the impact of the view and the subtle nuances of the changing light.

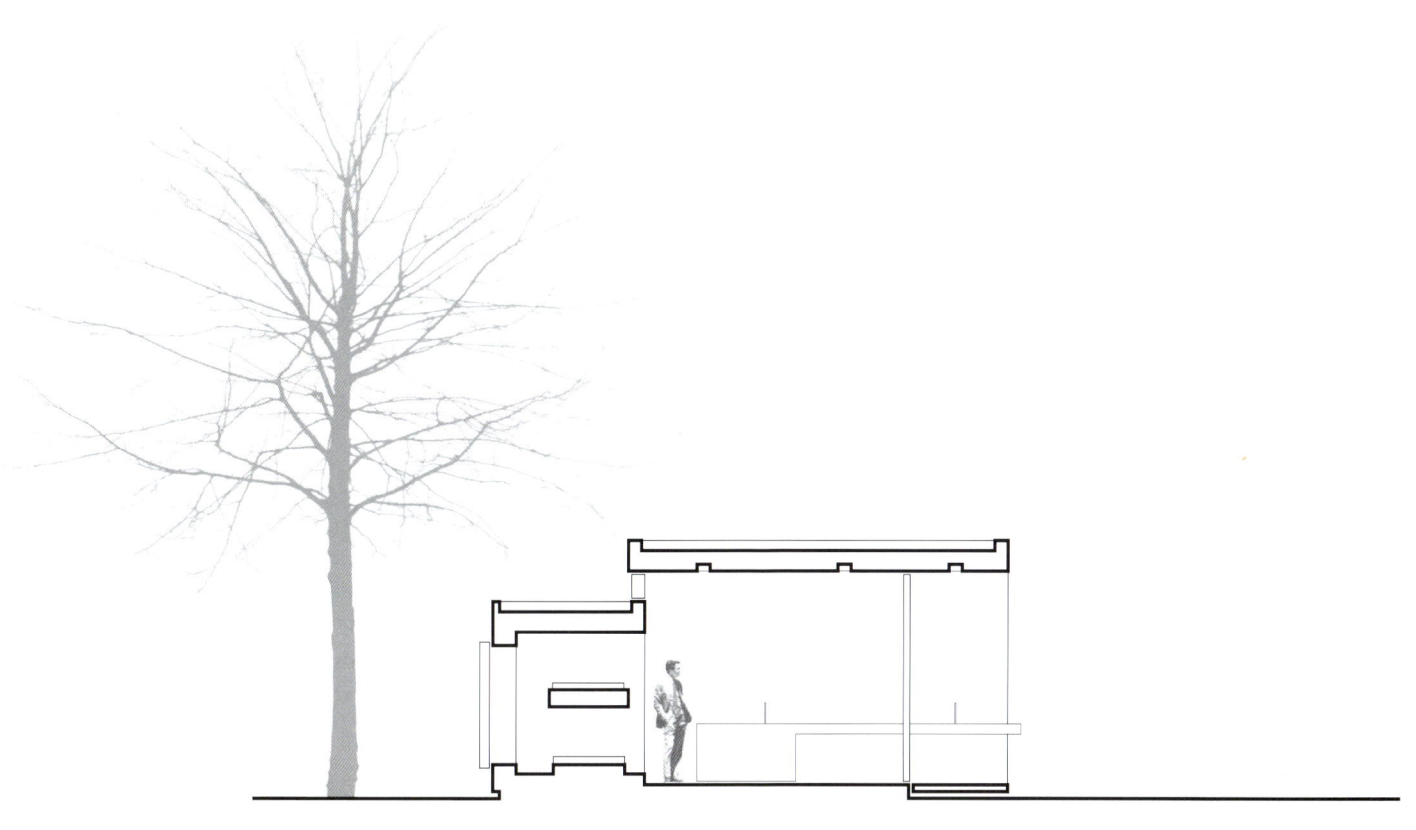

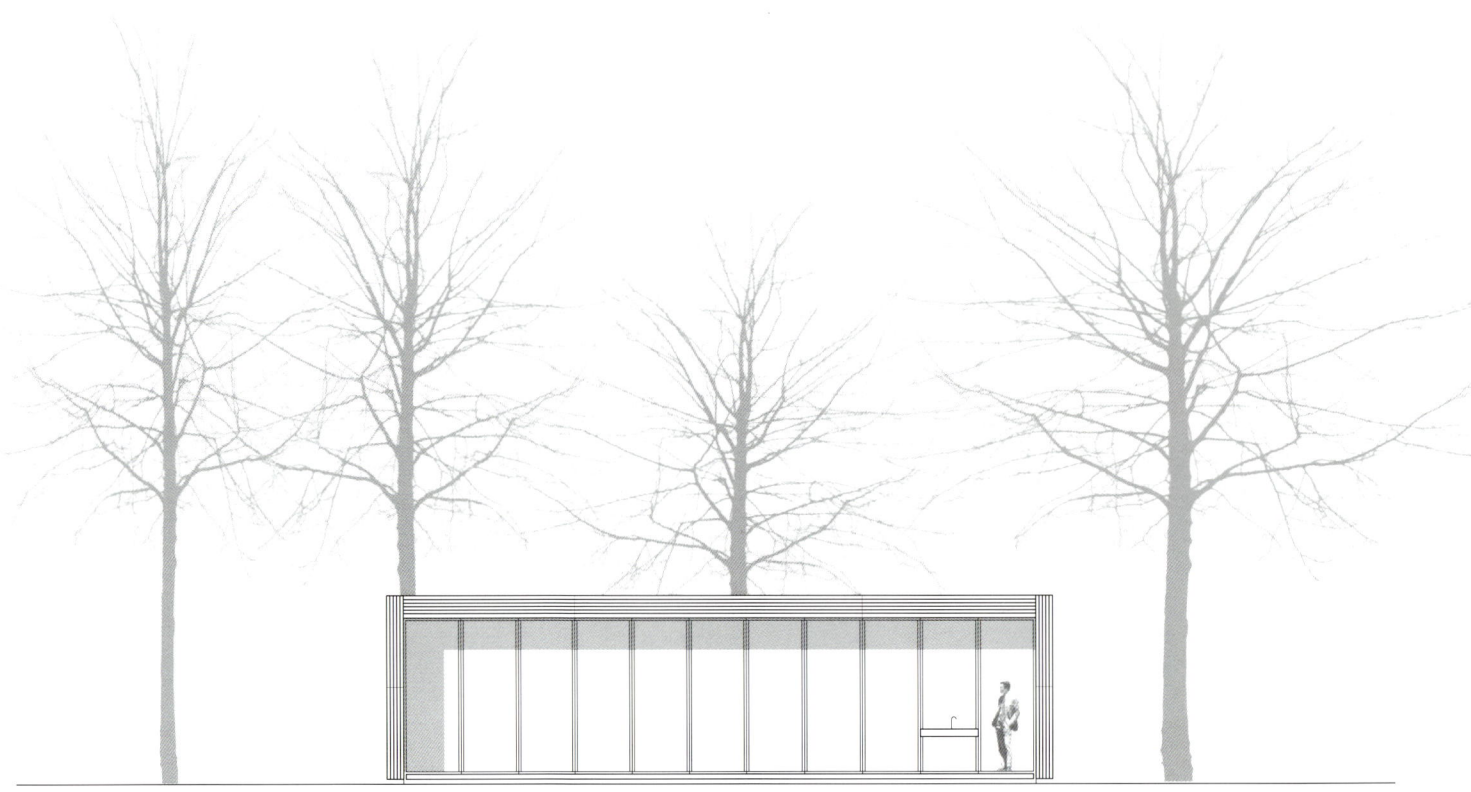

East elevation

Standing on the lawn outside the house, it is easy to get a clear sense of the cottage's informing idea. A Nordic summer evening, a deep blue sky topping the forest canopy - the large glass panels slid away and people relaxing on the patio, sitting at the long table. Beyond them, the annex's structure of tightly-integrated intimate spaces and, framing the whole, a density of green foliage.

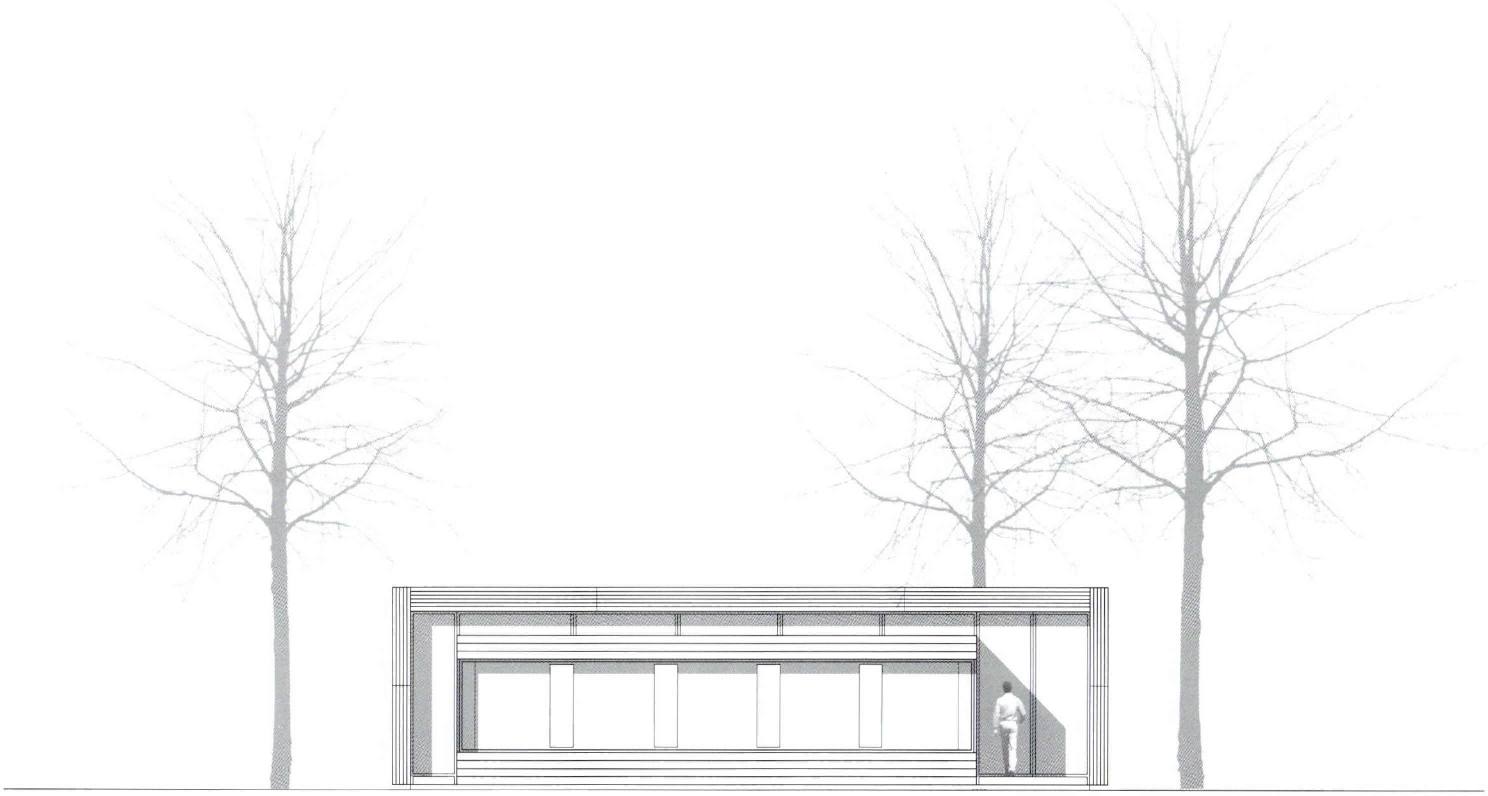

West elevation

Timber and glass preponderate. Slats and cladding in Siberian larch offer, inside and out, vertical and horizontal profiles, respectively - a refinement of the materiality of the wood, the summer cottage as wooden casket. Glass set in vertical frames of Oregon pine secures the open aspect. In conjunction with the rough-coated light-toned concrete of the kitchen table, the area of polished concrete flooring that in the main unit complements the wooden flooring offsets the warm accents of the timber.

The weeHouse team / Warner + Asmus

weeHouse

The motivation behind the pared down design of this house was a rejection of the trend in the US that bigger is better. The weeHouse, designed for Stephani Arado by Geoff Warner of Minnesota-based Alchemy Architects, is a study in efficient use of space. The contemporary cabin is a simple 12-foot by 24-foot rectangle with glass sides. It contains custom cabinetry, cantilevered shelves with sliding aluminum doors and two built-in beds. The weeHouse was built in response to Arado's limited budget, her desire to minimally impact the site, and to create a quiet space for retreat. The quality of space was more important than amenities (there is no electricity, running water, or sewer connection). It serves as a weekend getaway and is essentially a log cabin in the country. The location, a small plot on Minnesota farmland, was remote and lacking in basic facilities, so the house was prefabricated and transported whole. Instead of contracting out the work, Warner built the cabin himself, with the help of Lucas Alm and Scott McGlasson, both of whom share Warner's Minnesota office. The cabin took about eight weeks to complete, was trucked to the site, and hoisted onto its foundation by crane.

Location:
Minnesota, USA
Photographs:
Photographs: Warner + Asmus

The cabin is singular in style because of its simplicity, construction method and the fact that it was designed for its site. The weeHouse is Arado's prefabricated sanctuary, the place she goes whenever she wants to be peaceful.

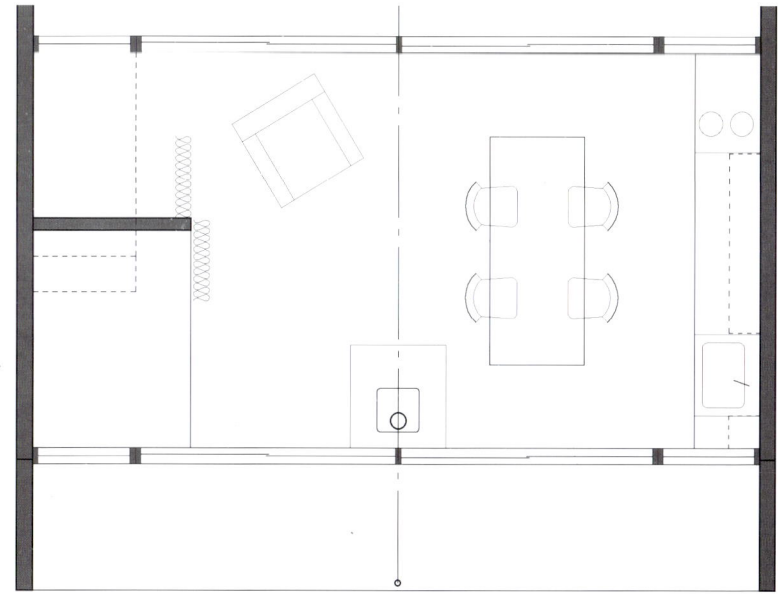

The floor plan is extremely simple: a 3.60x7.25 m rectangle with enough space for a kitchen and two beds placed against the wall. The rest of the furniture consists of made-to-measure wardrobes, projecting shelves with aluminum doors, a table for four and the chimney.

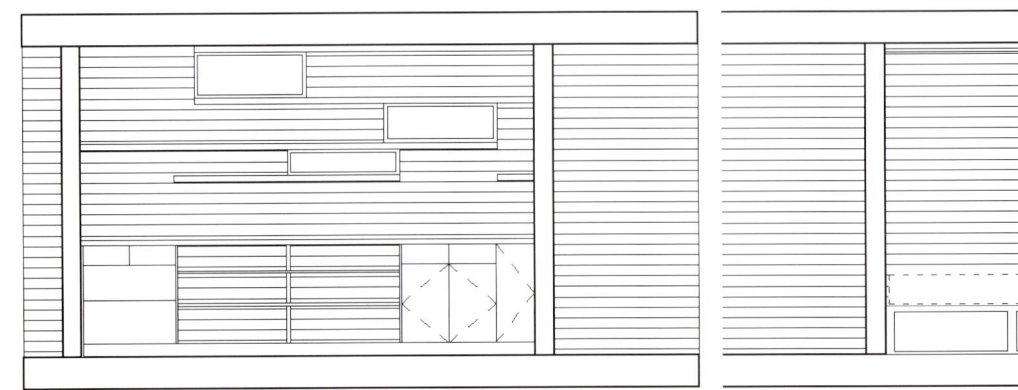

Kitchen elevation

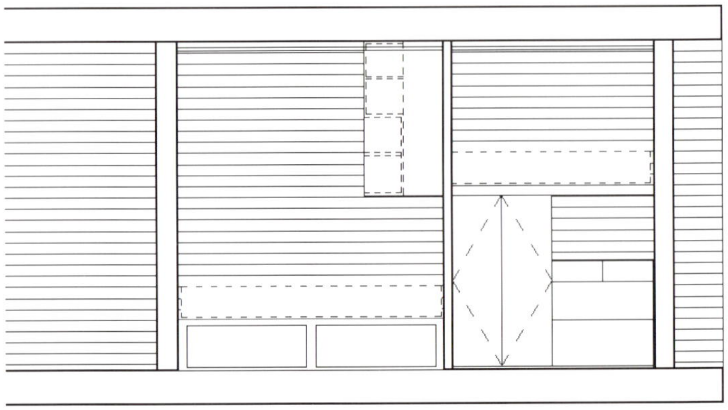

Bedroom elevation

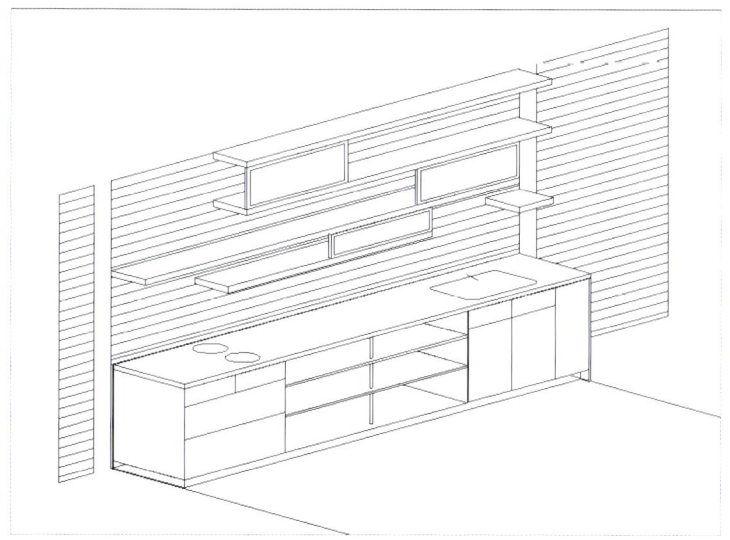
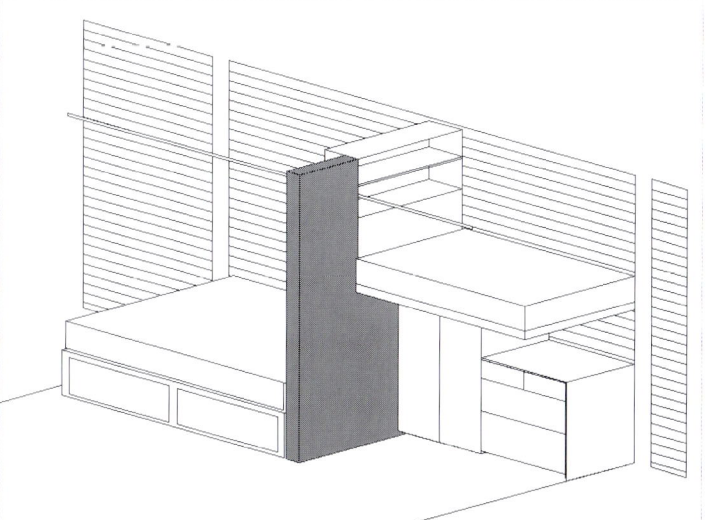

Rojkind arquitectos

PR 34 House

A refurbishment and an extension was required to an existing late 60s house, located in a residential area in Tecamachalco estado de México, on a hillside over looking Bosques de Las Lomas.
The house was carefully cleaned to achieve more open areas. Then a new part of the program was required, an independent apartment for the client's daughter.
Once entered through the garage the house divides into 2 parts with separate entrance, giving total independence to the addition which is accessed through a spiraling staircase 2 flights up.
Resembling a dance composed of 2 bodies in motion, the looping sensual from that changes angles coming up of every curve was inspired by the profession of the ballet dancer who is going to inhabit it.
Once you arrive at the apartment it is separated into 2 half levels, the first containing the kitchen dining and living area. Going down a half level we find the TV room and the master bedroom. Taking advantage of the roof of the existing house and its skylights, this roof becomes a terrace with remains of chipped lava rocks used for the main wall of the house. The skylights become acrylic stools, benches and chaise lounges that change color with a LED lighting system.
Making use of the extraordinary labor in Mexico, the structure is made out of 4" rolled steel beams, and the shell is made with 5mm steel plates that were carefully body shaped as if building a ship or a spacecraft. Underneath the steel plates, 2 layers of 1 ½" mineral wool fiber are used as thermal acoustic insulation. The interior is then covered with 9mm chipboard with an off-white resin finish.

Location:
Tecamachalco, Mexico
Photographs:
Jaime Navarro

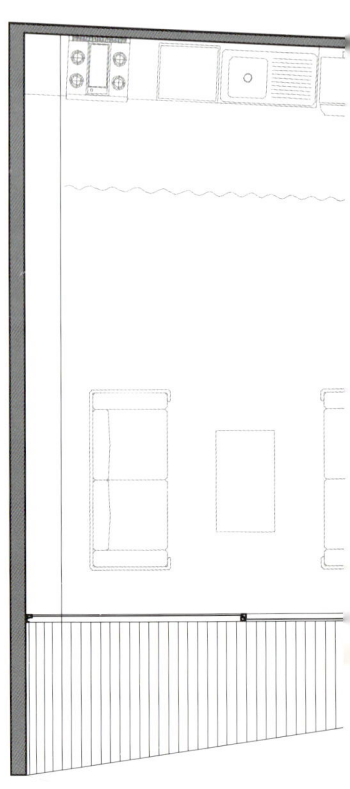
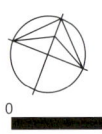

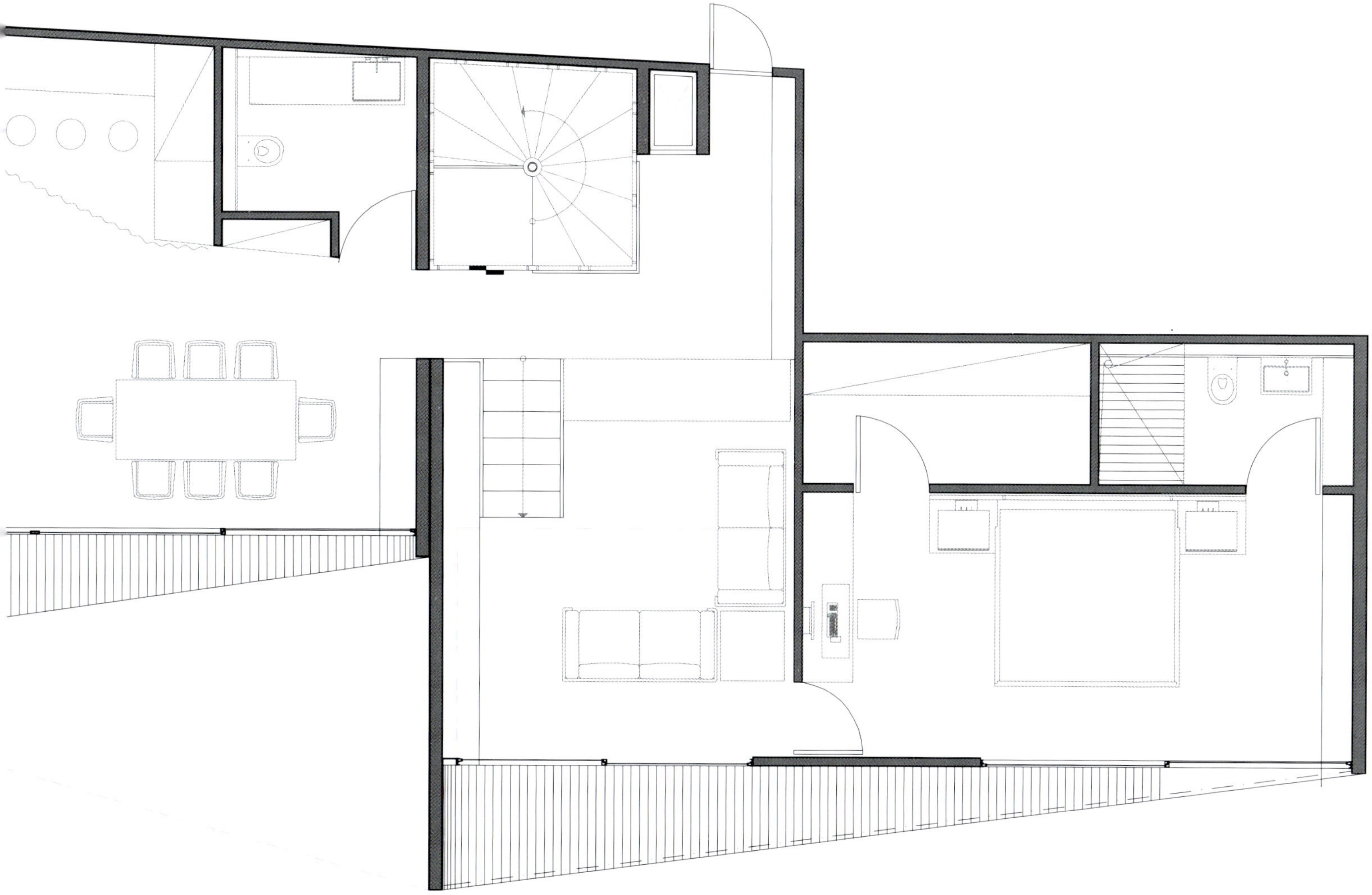

5

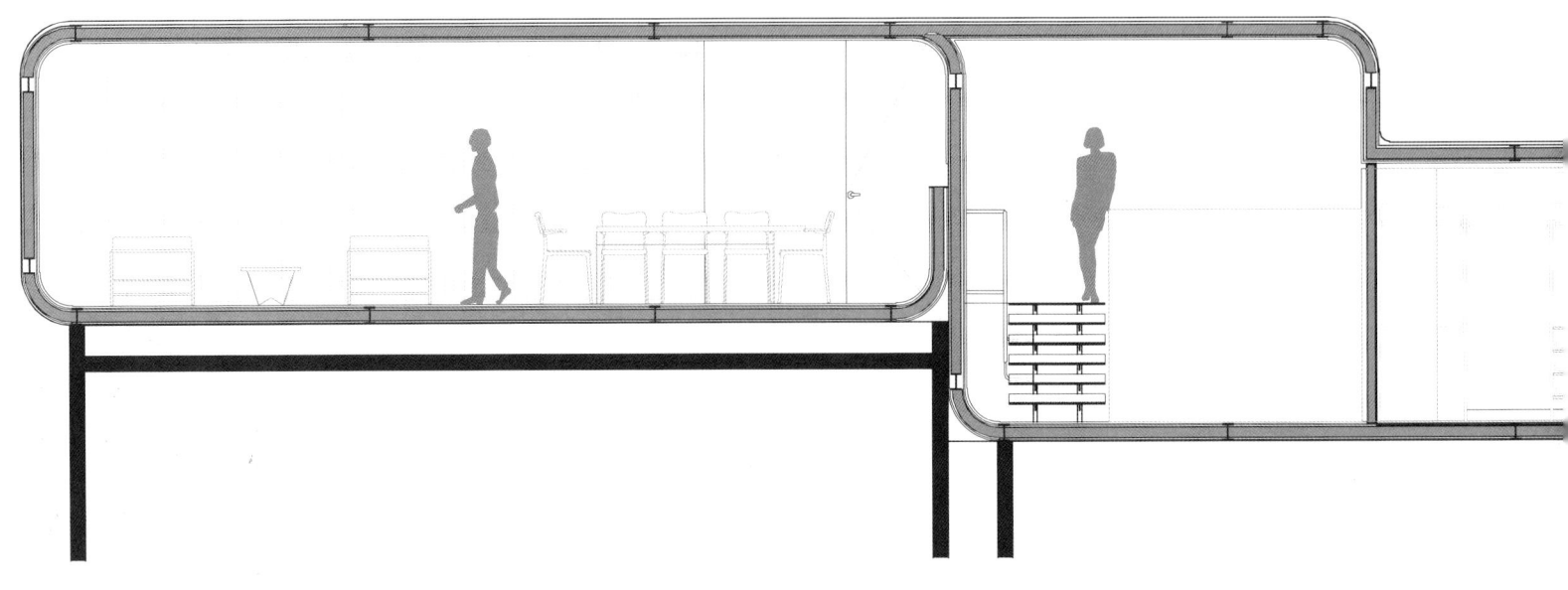
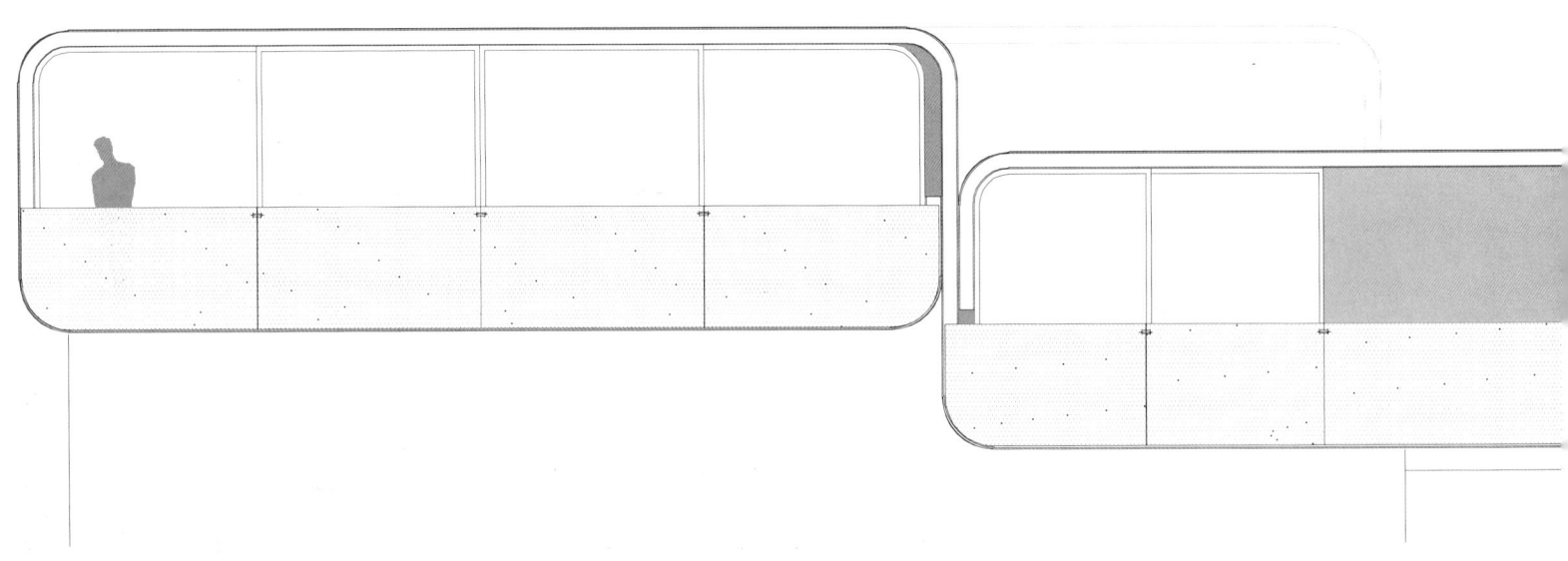

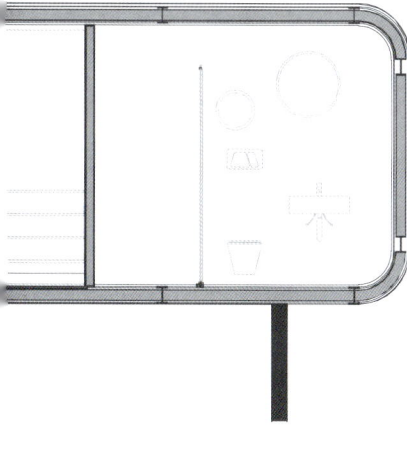

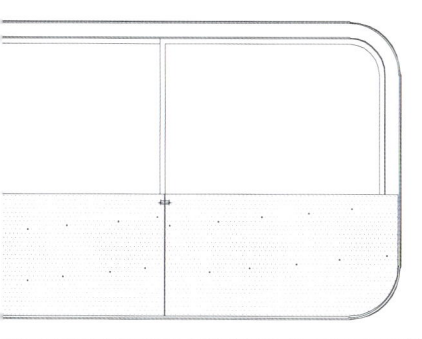

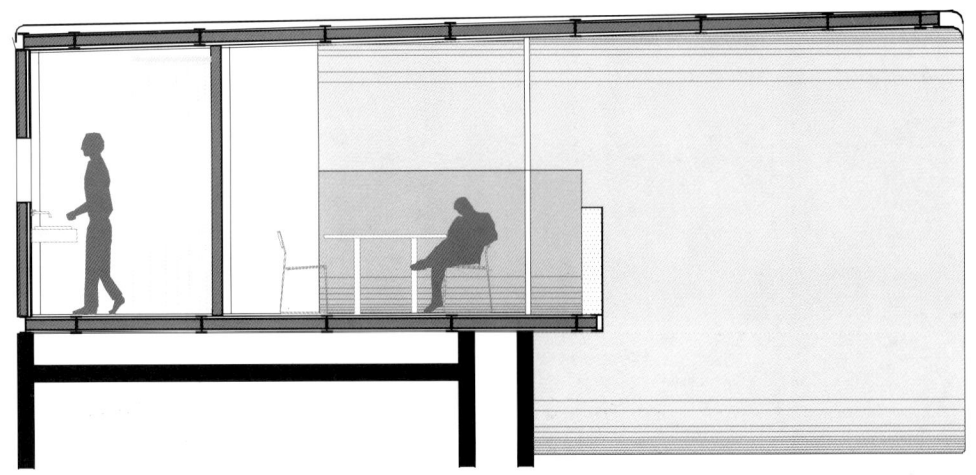

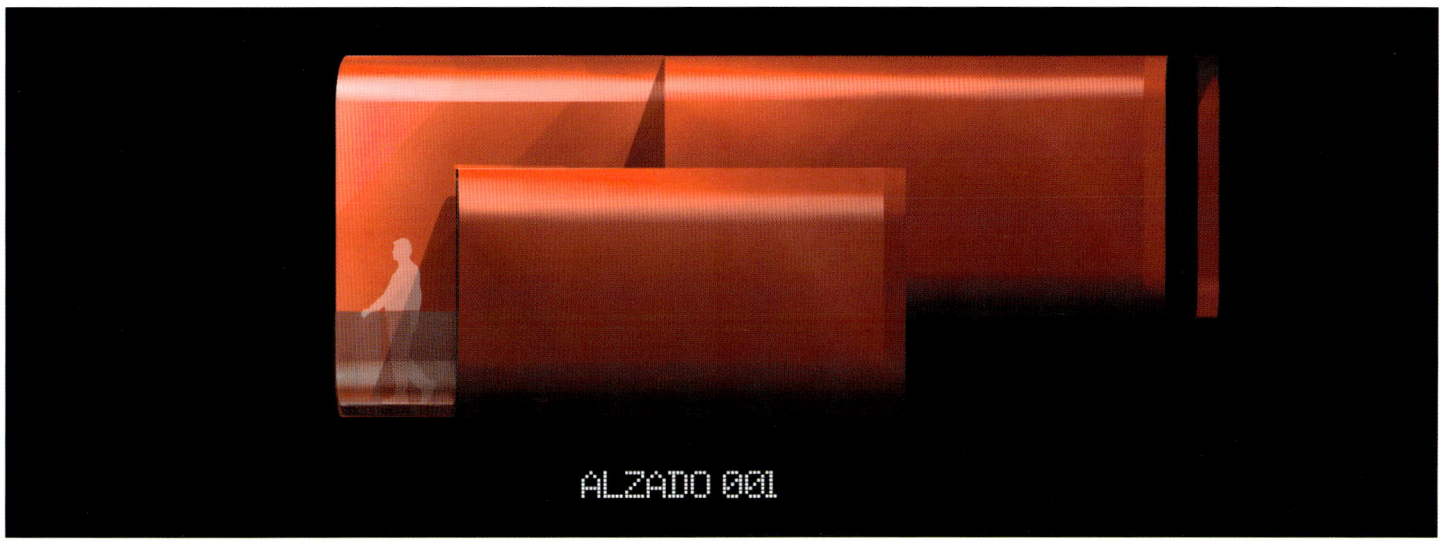

ALZADO 001

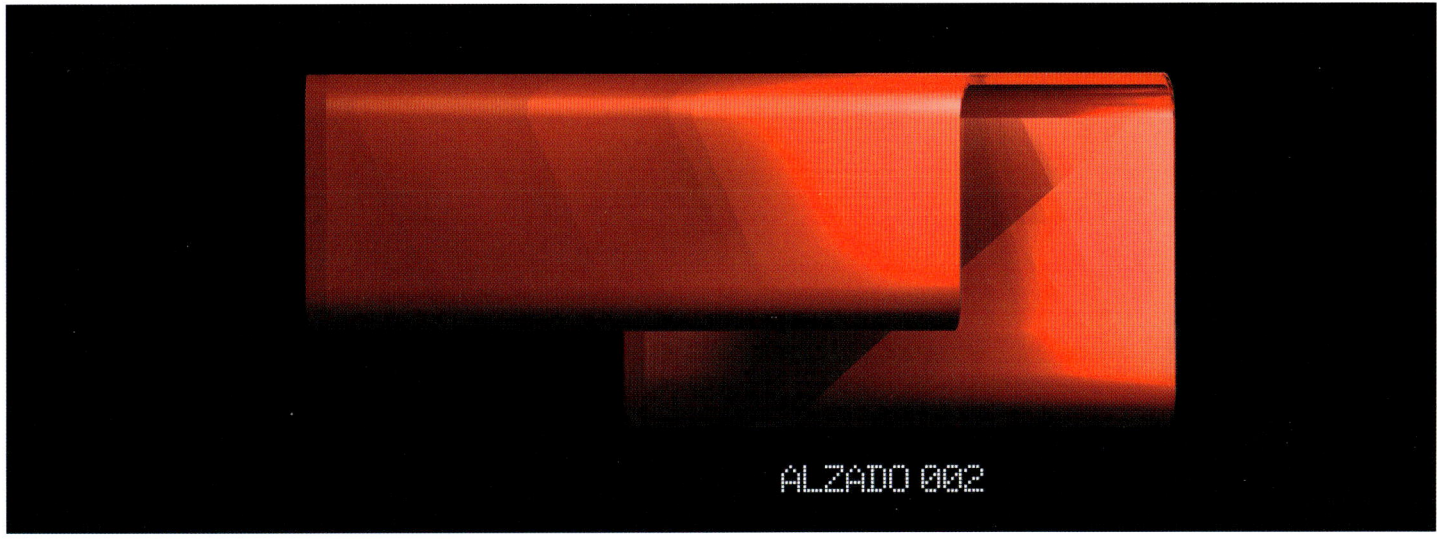

ALZADO 002

Rafael Iglesia

House on the Riverside

This house is built in an area where history is short and space immense, and people inhabit geography more than history. Their environment is vastness, and it is the landscape that shapes them and makes them fellow countrymen. On the Paraná River, the horizon - which divides the earth from the heavens - is defined by a line thicker than a raised hand. The house is built on four levels: the street-level entrance; a green zone that conceals what goes on a few meters below; the swimming pool; and the roof, which is also the largest living space. Below this, the house and further down, the riverside wharf. The focal point of the project is the patio, between the swimming pool wall and the house. From here the river is still visible through the glass walls, which form a huge window as wide as the living space behind them. This house is a pool pavilion. The full potential of water is perceived by the senses from the cascade that defines one of its sides. It is not only seen but also heard as it falls; its spray can be smelled on the lawn and, above all, changes of temperature can be sensed and felt.

The building is pure structure. As in his other buildings, the architect sought to intensify the discharge of natural forces and make them more complex. The structure complicates the path of gravity, that imaginary line that links objects to the earth by the shortest possible route.

The beams are displaced: either inverted to frame the landscape in a particular way, or placed so as to protect the building from the western sun and modify the scale. From the interior, the displaced beams interfere with the perception of stability, while on the outside they blend into the horizon. The building's only language is the one that sustains it. It is like the towns and villages in the vastness of this landscape: a meteorite fallen from the sky, a rock tossed into a field.

Location:
Barranca del Paraná, Argentina

Photographs:
contributed by the architect

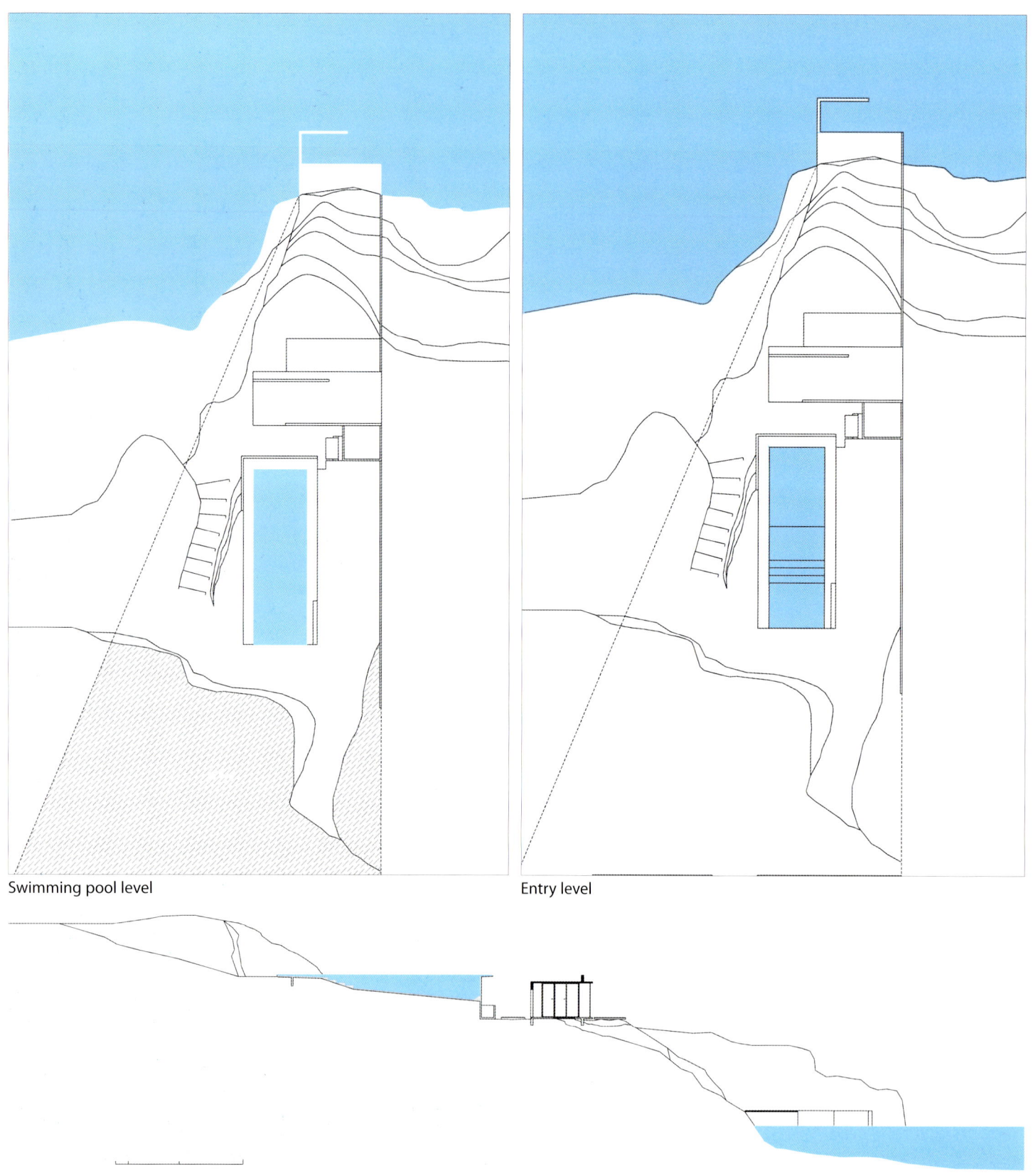

Swimming pool level

Entry level

Dwelling level

The cascade that defines one of the pavilion walls exemplifies the architect's search for a sensual architecture that doesn't exclude smells, sounds, movement, vistas, echoes. Shadows, sounds and reflections are not predefined but produced by the structure.

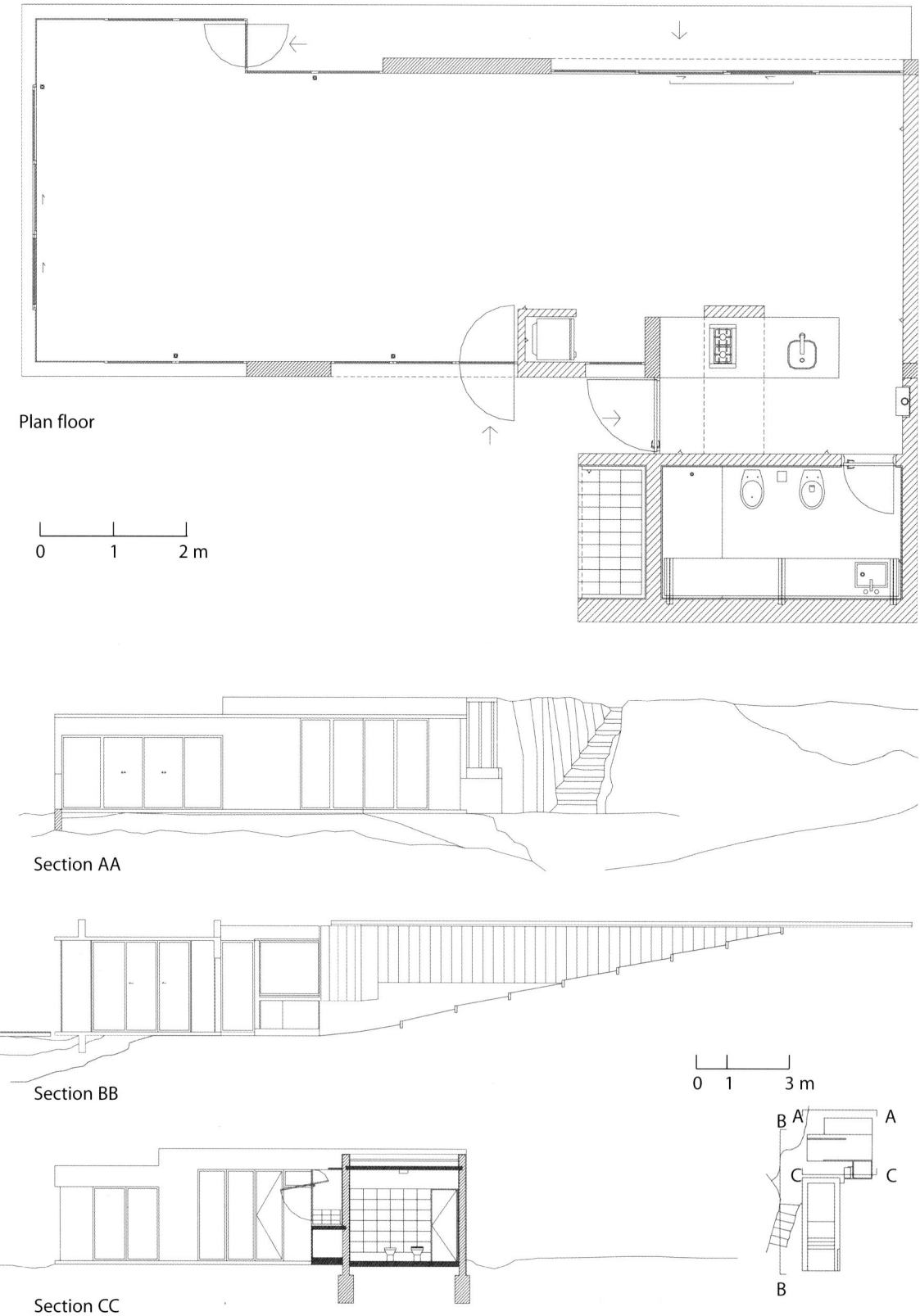

Plan floor

0 1 2 m

Section AA

Section BB

Section CC

0 1 3 m

Atelier Bow - Wow

Asama House

This site is located on the edge of the famous mountain resort Karuizawa, 2 hours by car from Tokyo. Since it borders farm land, the area is a mixture of holiday homes and farm houses. To the west are rice paddies and to the east is forest. The project is a simple, single room for a family and is surrounded by 15-meter-high trees. All the living spaces directly benefit from the daily shifts of natural light and views of the canopy of trees surrounding the home. The building is square in plan, with a pyramidal roof. The issue for this project was how to affect the purity of this form with the specific nature of the various orientations.

The ceiling space is divided into 5 portions by suspended walls giving a suggestion of rooms. The suspended walls act as large beams so that columns are not required, and a single space can be maintained below.

The position of the suspended walls is determined by the combination of proportions to suit activities such as dining, living, studying, sleeping and washing. The angles of the roof planes are also defined by these proportions.

The architects made every effort to incorporate the site's abundant light into the scheme. While the trunk-scape of the forest is framed, the tops of the trees with a backdrop of blue sky are pulled into the space by large openings. By planning the layout in this way, each of the 9 external surfaces of the house obtained an opening. The light qualities entering through each of these openings measure changing time, seasons and orientation. At sunset, a particular portion of the ceiling space becomes stained in a changing hue of orange, while the other portions show various shades of gray.

Location:
Kariuzawa, Japan

Photographs:
Atelier Bow - Wow

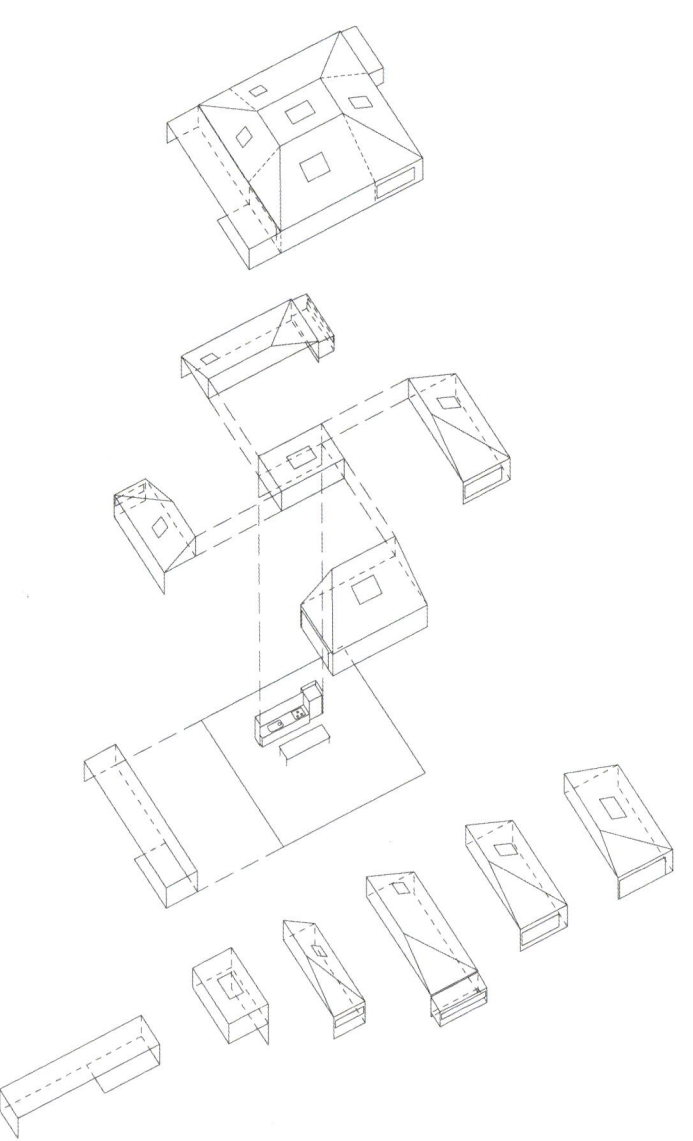

The design of the suspended walls eliminates the need for structural beams, while implying the division of the space below into "rooms".

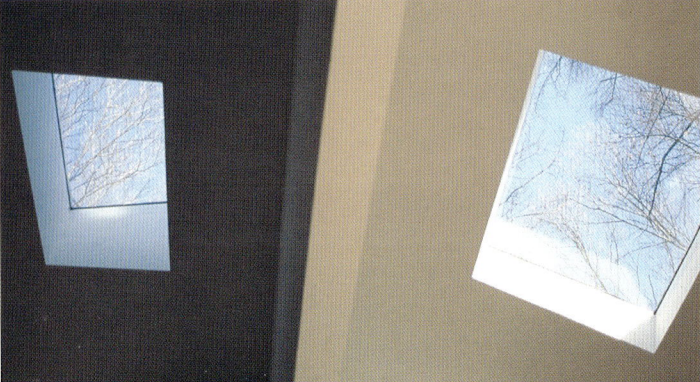

The roof has been broken up into five planes, each facing in a different direction and each punctuated by a skylight. These skylights, along with the ample openings on each façade, ensure that the interior enjoys abundant changing light throughout the day.

Ground floor plan
1. Terrace
2. Living room
3. Study
4. Bedroom
5. Lavatory
6. Dining room

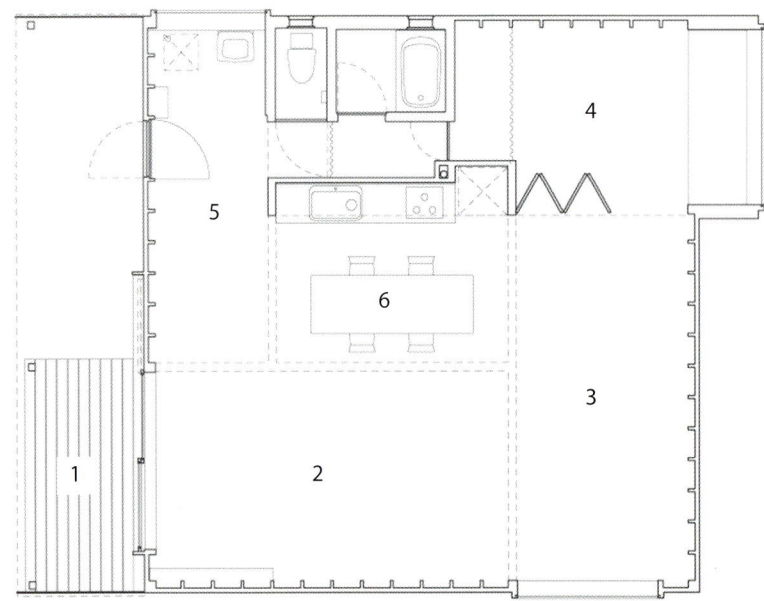

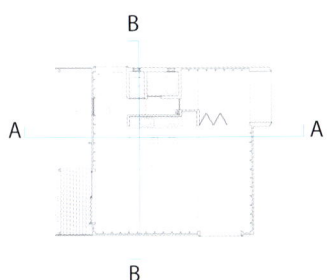

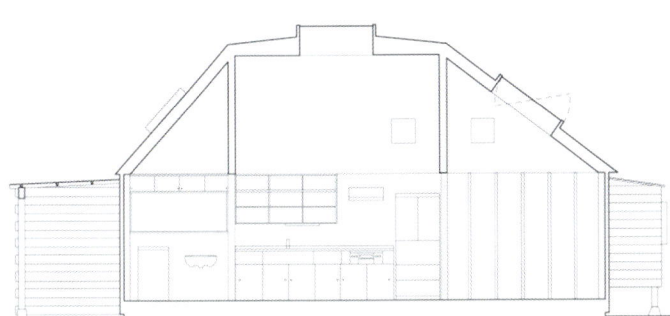

Section AA

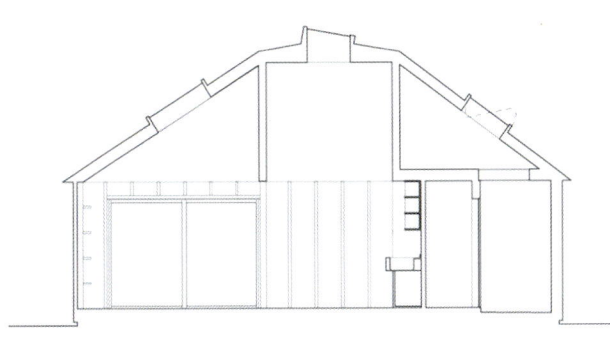

Section BB

North elevation

East elevation

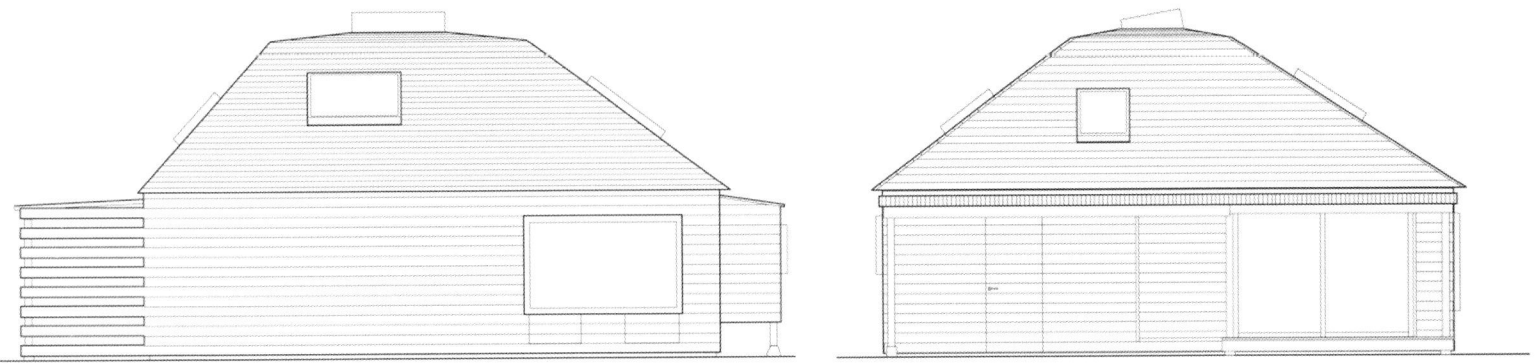

South elevation

West elevation

1. Galvanized and aluminum coated steel sheet, t=0.4; asphalt roofing; structural plywood, t=9
2. Plasterboard t=9.5 AEP; ceiling joist; glass wool
3. Structural plywood, t=9 AEP; furring strip
4. Lauan plywood; ceiling joist; glass wool
5. Cedar t=12; asphalt roofing; furring strip; glass wool
6. Structural plywood; floor joist
7. Flexible board t=6 AEP; furring strip
8. Flexible board t=6 AEP; lauan plywood; waterproofing sheet; furring strip
9. Stud: Western hemlock
10. Lauan plywood; structural plywood; styrofoam; floor joist
11. Styrofoam, vaporproof sheet; concrete sub-slab; crushed stone

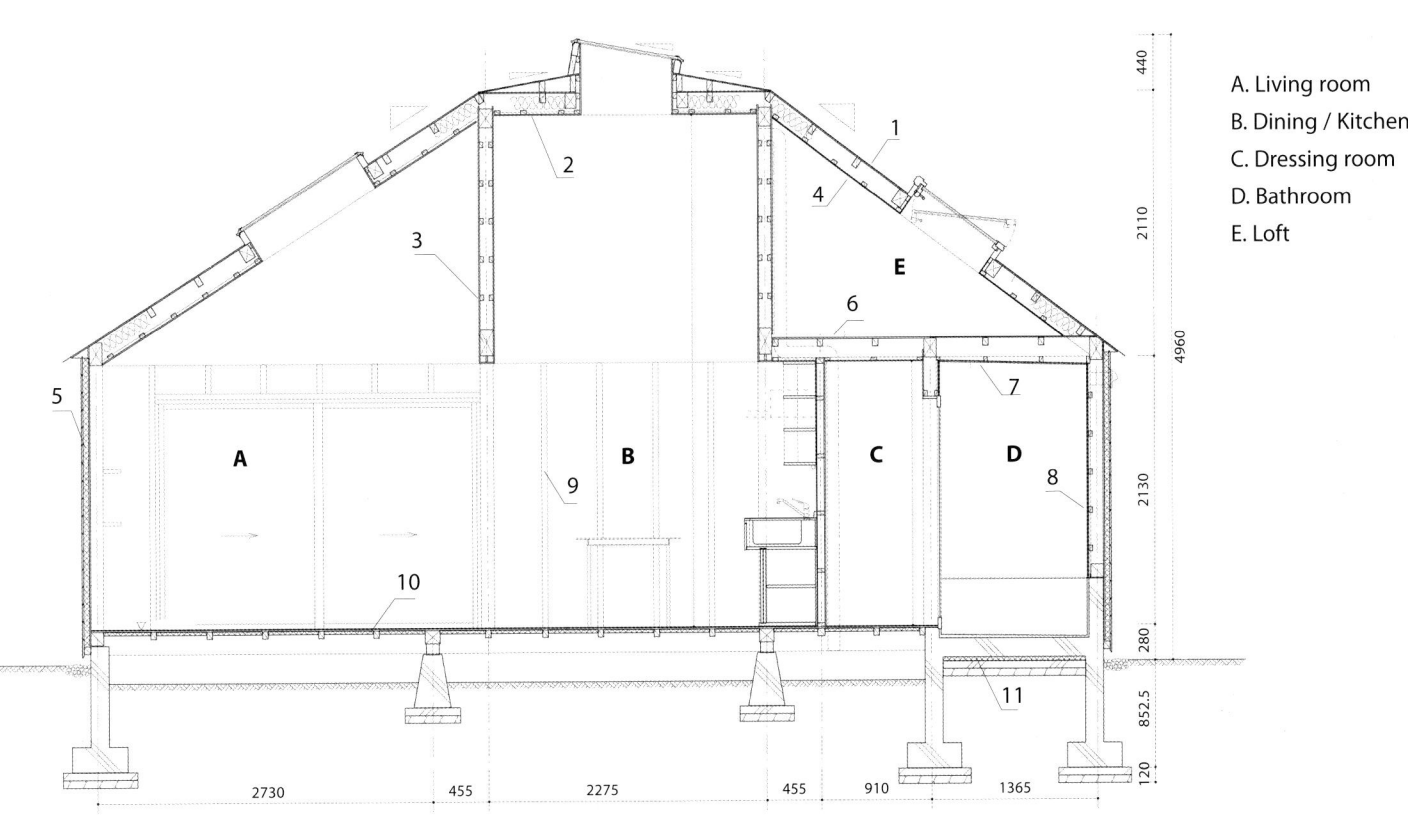

A. Living room
B. Dining / Kitchen
C. Dressing room
D. Bathroom
E. Loft

55

Takaharu + Yui Tezuka / Tezuka Architects, Masahiro Ikeda / mias

Engawa House

The Engawa House was designed to accommodate a single family. To the north of the site is the grandparents' home, with the eldest son and his family living on the second floor. The building-to-land ratio in the area is high and most houses take up the entire surface of properties, leaving no space for a garden. The grandparents' home was no exception, with its southern engawa (a multifunctional space which roughly corresponds to the veranda) facing a massive wall at a distance of only 50 centimeters. That is precisely where their daughter and her husband decided to settle when by chance the southern lot was put up for sale.

Plans were thus laid out for a long, narrow building bordering the south road. An open area along the northern side would provide space for an inner garden, which, being set alongside a low, one-story house, would receive plenty of light. The southern roadside wall was erected to a height of 2.2 meters, with a high-side opening that would protect the family's privacy while giving a clear view of the sky. On the other side, floor-to-ceiling windows provide a full perspective of the garden. The result is a 16.2-meter-long and 4.6-meter-wide space encased between two L-shaped frames.

Wood was chosen as the main construction material because it ensures a monolithic sense of unity, but the length of the openings meant that reinforcements had to be added. The difference in height of the northern and southern openings gives the whole structure an unusual appearance, like uneven parallel bars. Visual lines are interrupted, but the space itself was conceived as one single volume.

Nine sliding doors allow the house to open completely on the garden side. And so when a group of family and friends gathered at a garden party to celebrate the completion of the building, the idea naturally arose that the whole structure resembled an engawa.

Location: Tokyo, Japan
Photographs: Katsuhisa Kida

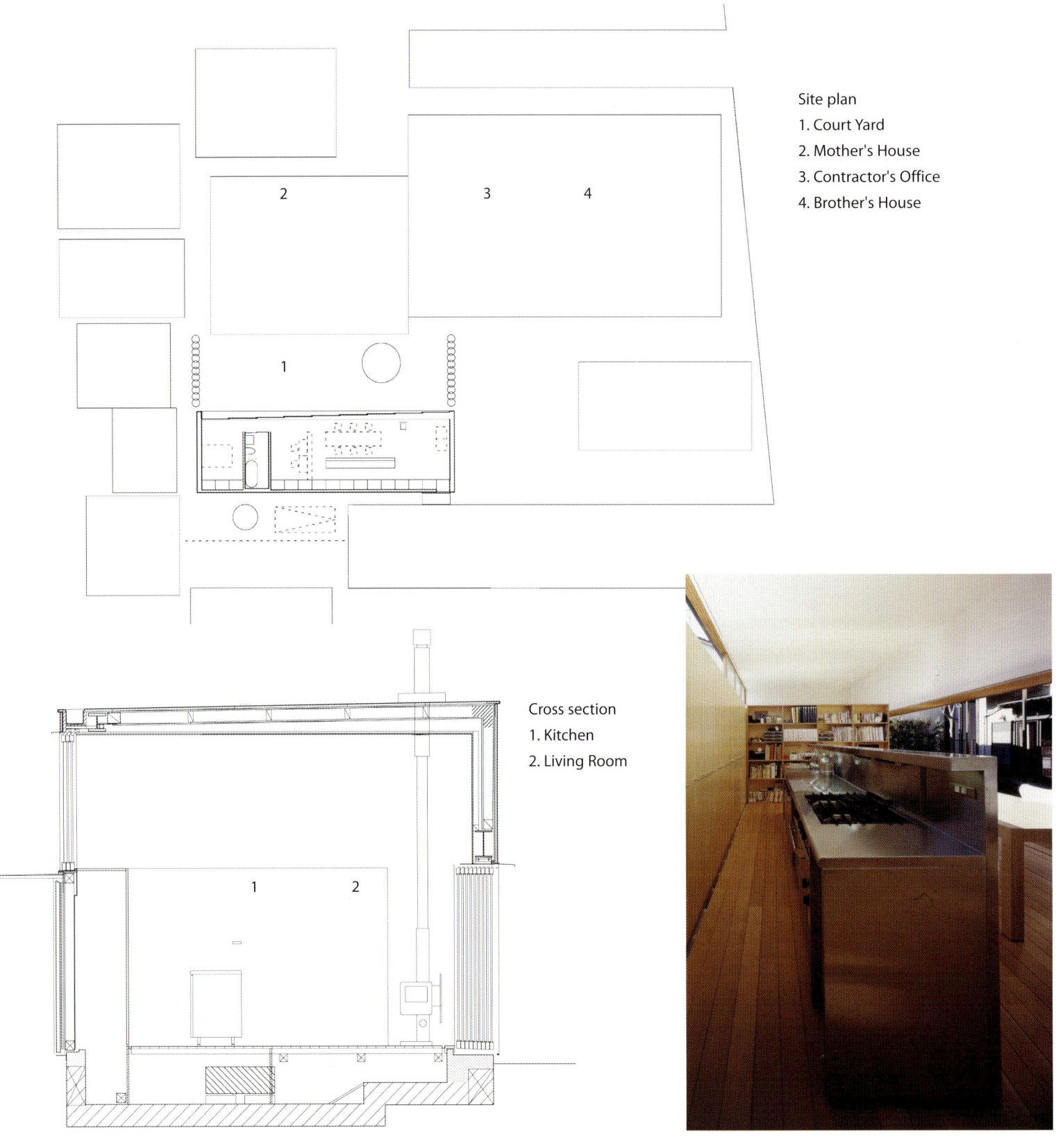

Site plan
1. Court Yard
2. Mother's House
3. Contractor's Office
4. Brother's House

Cross section
1. Kitchen
2. Living Room

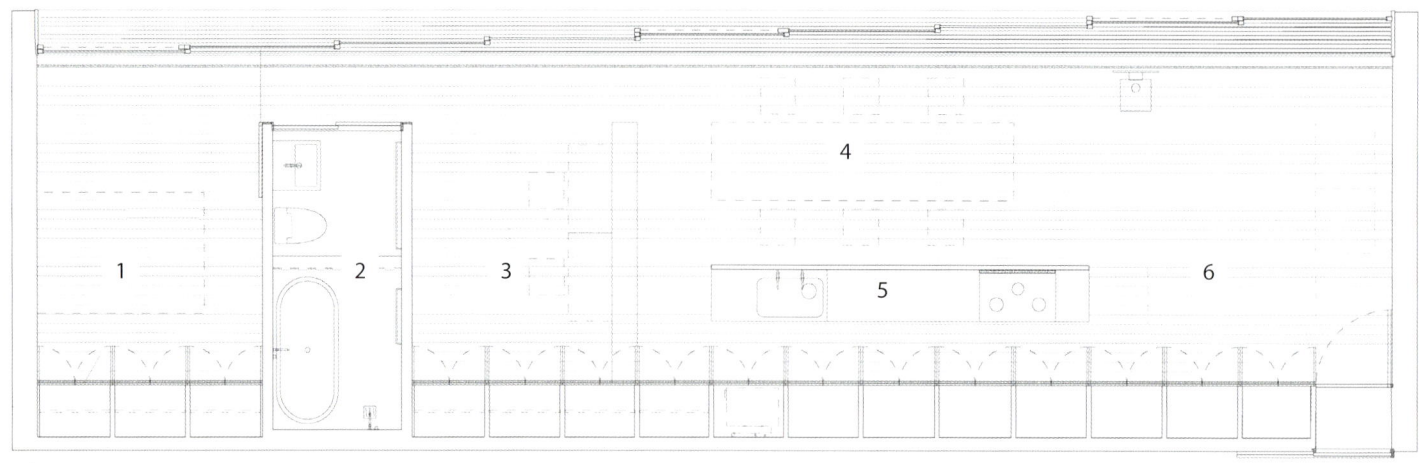

Floor plan
1. Master Bedroom
2. Bathroom
3. Children's Room
4. Dining Room
5. Kitchen
6. Living Room

While the dividing walls reach a height of two meters, the roof is three and a half meters high, making the air throughout subject to similar conditions. For example, steam rising from the bathtub dissolves into the warm and voluminous space, compensating for the dryness of Japanese winters. The kitchen was conceived without an extractor hood, nor were ventilating fans necessary, since the difference in height of the northern and southern openings creates a natural airflow. In the summer, hot air rises toward the roof and naturally exits through the high-side opening.

Bellemo & Cat

Cocoon House

The house is called "Cocoon" not because it looks like a cocoon, (it actually looks more like a Zeppelin and was built using a mixture of timber boat building techniques and aircraft technology) but because it functions as a cocoon, "both as a nascent Architectural firm and as a family", for the architects who designed it for their own recreational use. The site itself is on a very steep plot of land with spectacular views as well as excessive exposure to harsh weather conditions. Thus, the design scheme had to simultaneously shield the home from inclement weather while at the same time opening the interior to the view. The end result is a pod-like structure that allows for adequate insulation on all sides of the building except those facing the most desirable views.

Seeming to float amidst the trees, this steel-clad, boat-like cocoon holds in its belly a large glass-faced plywood rectangle facing the westerly ridge of the hills and the ocean. Large sliding doors open this volume out toward the trees, giving the sense of being both inside and out at the same time. The more pragmatic, square-shaped laundry and bathroom areas are located just past this space, while two sleeping cabins are nestled in the "hull", their walls assuming the ovoid shape of the exterior.

Structurally inspired by boat and aircraft building technology, a rectangular structure was built first to house the living and washing areas, later adding a series of plywood ribs to create the shape. Green hardwood battens conforming to the basic shape were then applied, thus creating a monocoque fuselage-style structure. Colorbond shingles form the final exterior skin, serving at once as cladding and structural reinforcement.

The rooms at the ends have no standard post and beam structure, relying instead on the mesh of the timber battens and shingles to form a strong, structural shell.

The building process itself was something of a challenge. Because the plot was so steep and prone to landslides, the builders had to work with climbing ropes and harnesses. Standard scaffolding was out of the question (again, due to the slope) and the round hull of the structure meant that there was no roof to stand on. To overcome this, the ceiling beams and floor joists were left jutting out of the building to be used as secure platforms from which to work.

The exterior cladding of this totally ovoid building required a durable yet lightweight and flexible material. The solution was simple: customizing a standard BHP Colorbond flat sheet into shingles.

Considering its relative low cost and ease of construction (not on this site perhaps, but in a factory) the architects are contemplating prototyping the house as a possible prefab housing model. They are also working on a fabric skin and exposed skeleton.

Location: Wye River, Southern Victoria, Australia
Photographs: Mark Munro

Longitudinal section

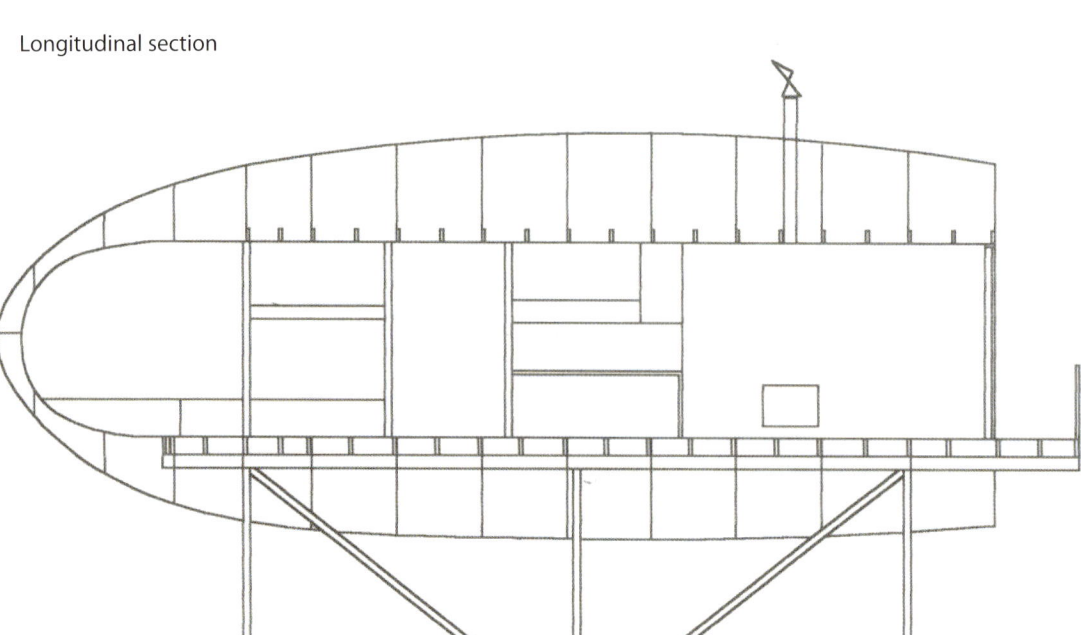

Structurally inspired by boat and aircraft building technology, a rectangular structure was built first to house the living and washing areas, later adding a series of plywood ribs to create the shape.

Ground floor plan
1. Entry
2. Living
3. Dining
4. Kitchen
5. Bathroom
6. Laundry / wc
7. Bunk beds
8. Main bedroom
9. Deck

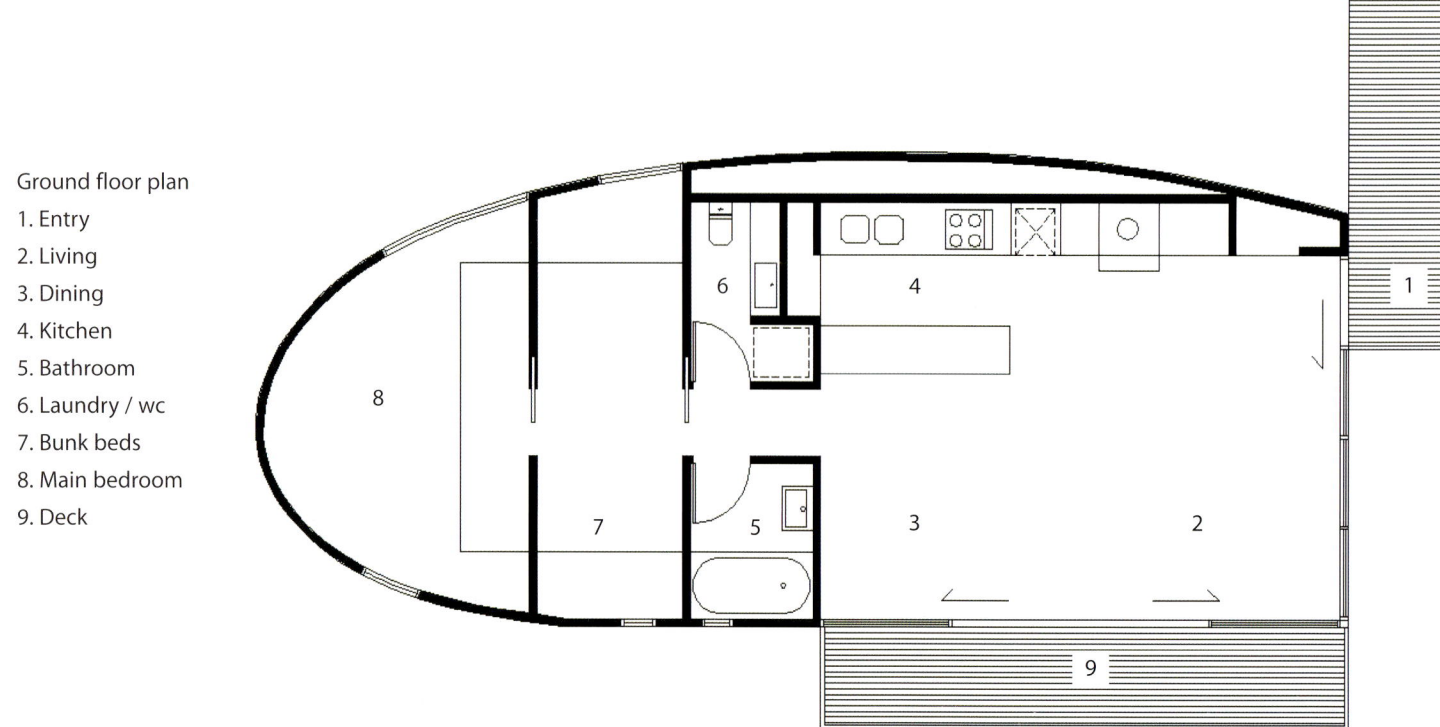

Denton & Corker & Marshall

Marshall House

This is a weekend holiday house overlooking a small bay two hours east of Melbourne. Buried into the dunes, the house is visible from the beach as a low black line - the color of the rocks - with ragged tufts of dune grass above it. It is completely hidden from the landward side. The objective was to maintain a low profile and to have an internal focus to the house, avoiding engagement with the surrounding context.

The house is a long thin concrete box, black inside and out, set along one edge of a large square courtyard contained by three-meter-high black concrete walls with dune berms ramped up to roof level on three sides. On the open ocean elevation, windows are sized and positioned within each room to act as picture frames to the views, and the proportions and locations of the windows are determined by these internal considerations. The courtyard offers protection from winds and is a north facing sun trap in winter.

The house in no-way connotes a residence or domesticity. In its context it lurks like a Stealth bomber, hidden and subversive.

Location:
Phillip Island, Victoria, Australia
Photographs:
John Gollings

80

81

Main elevation

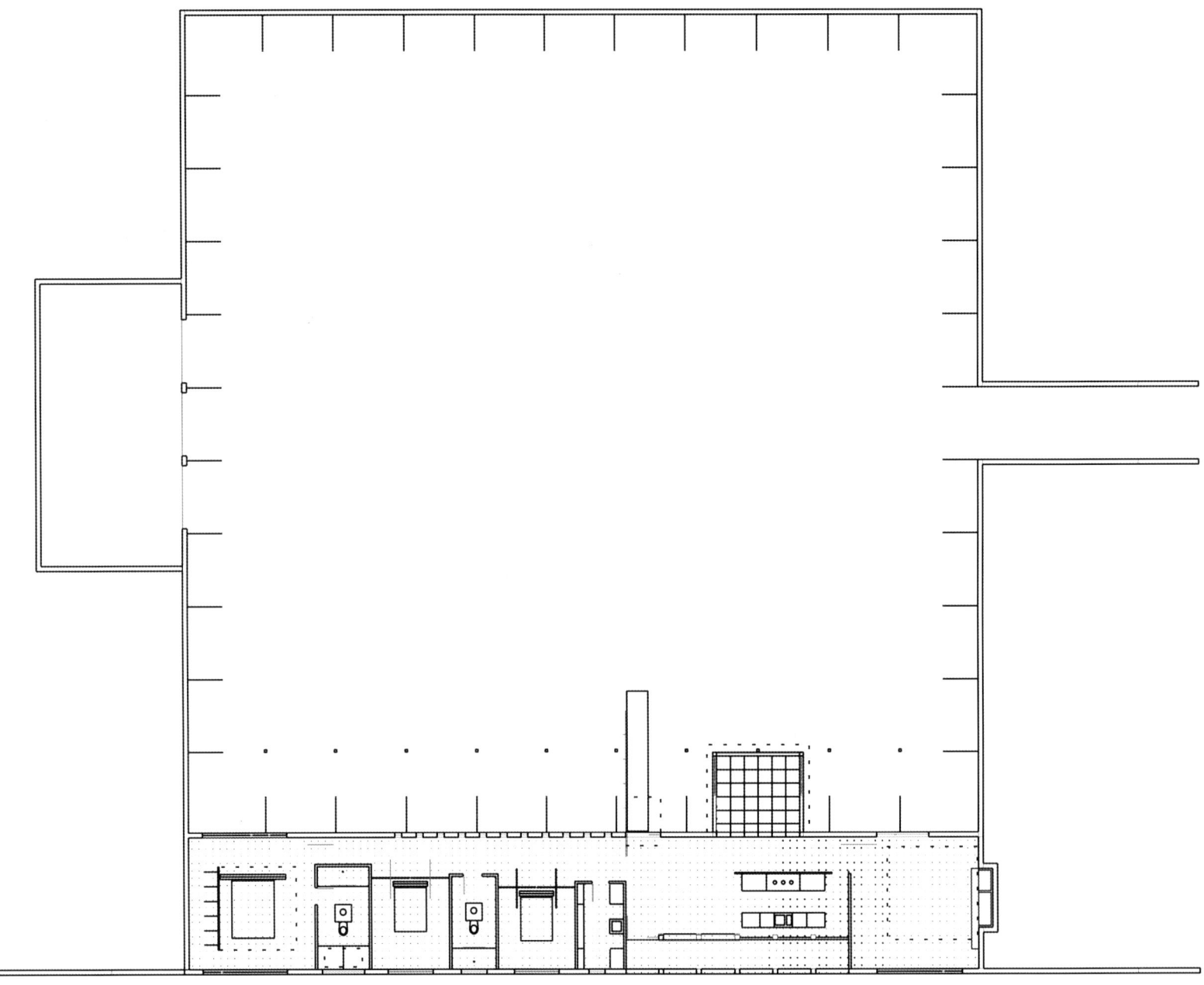

Ground floor plan

Windows are sized and positioned within each room to act as picture frames to the views.

Peter Hulting Architect
Meter Arkitektur
Guest Appearance

When Swedish architect Peter Hulting was asked to transform this old farm site into a couple's new home, he immediately saw the potential to create an unpretentious, sensitive space with the ability to connect both to its immediate surroundings and the neighboring open landscape. Specific only in their demands for a concrete floor and clay roof tiles, quality craftsmanship and simplicity were key to the couple's vision of "a house that could age with dignity".

Walking into this small summer house situated on Sweden's west coast peninsula, you are immediately struck by a sense of space that belies its 538 square feet (50 sq m) of floor space. Everything from the furniture to the lighting has been designed to enhance the building's shape and size - from the elongated Japanese-style table and benches, to the long steel-pipe chimney that guides the eye upwards from the open fire to the wooden ceiling. A combination of wood, concrete and plaster creates a range of tactile surfaces that compare and contrast in equal measure. The smooth concrete floor incorporates the water-carried heating system, while the use of sawed larch tree for the exterior walls and reclaimed clay tiles on the roof allow the building to sit perfectly within this picturesque setting.

In order to maximize on the available space, Hulting opted for an open plan design. By creating a large glass frontage overlooking the south-facing landscape, sliding doors define the inner space when required, while at the same time ensuring the interior of the guesthouse remains cool in the summer.

Creating compact solutions in such a reduced space was central to the design concept; this was achieved, in part, by allowing the dividing walls to work like large pieces of furniture within the main space. Towards one end a wardrobe doubles as a wall divider, separating the sleeping area from the rest of the house. The reverse of this wardrobe doubles as a set of bookshelves at the foot of the bed. There is also space for two loft beds here, while the simple design of Ulf Scherlin's "Birå 4" cupboard ensures that any clutter is neatly stored away out of sight. To the left of the bedroom, two sliding doors conceal the toilet and shower areas. The floors, tiled in Portuguese stone, offset standard white tiles that have been 'brick-mounted' and finished with a dark grey grout.

The kitchen sits in a semi-recess, cleverly defining its parameters without encroaching on the open-plan design of the overall space. The stainless steel of the kitchen contrasts beautifully with brightly colored handmade Portuguese tiles.

Location: Gothenburg, Sweden
Photographs: James Silverman

The shape of the dining table and benches add to the sense of space. Large sliding glass doors capitalize on the view and provide easy access to the exterior deck.

Takaharu+Yui Tezuka / Tezuka Architects, Masahiro Ikeda / Masahiro Ikeda co.,ltd

Roof House

The clients' brief for this small house (with a total floor area of 1044 sq ft or 97 sq m) had one unconventional requirement: they wanted to make full use of the entire roof surface. When the architects first went to meet with the clients at what was their residence at the time, they were immediately shown upstairs through a small window and onto a sharply pitched roof measuring only 65 sq ft (6 sq m). "We have lunch on this roof every day," they explained. Seeing such a limited space on such a sharply pitched roof, the architects decided to not only accommodate the needs of their clients, but also to push the possibilities of their dream.

Located in the suburbs of Tokyo, the Roof House in Hadano district, Kanagawa Prefecture splits the living spaces between the ground floor and the entire roof. By maintaining a simple plan and utilizing a lightweight, yet earthquake responsive structure, the house provides a visually and tactilely generous space for the family. The thin roof, timber columns, and structural plywood panels allow for a flexible, partitioned space and open the view through the house and out toward the nearby valley and Mt. Kobo.

The partitioned spaces are also organized with eight skylights above each room, serving specific family members: the younger sister's skylight above the children's room, the elder sister's skylight above the study room, the father's skylight above the bedroom, the mother's skylight above the kitchen, and the family's skylight above the dining room. A light bulb and lantern further complement this lighting configuration to respond to nighttime activities.

Climbing up the ladders that can be propped against the ledges of each skylight, the living space extends onto the rooftop and merges with the exterior. With a freestanding wall to break the wind and provide privacy, the rooftop is equipped with a dining table, benches, a kitchen, a stove, and even a shower. The 1 to 10 pitched roof provides a comfortable and identical slope to that of the original topography and has a low roof edge to further connect the roof life to the garden life, and facilitate, for example, passing barbecue platters up from the garden. This free-flow experience and expanded usable space not only keeps the family in contact with nature, but enriches life indoors.

Location:
Tokyo, Japan

Lighting designer:
Masahide Kakudate / Masahide Kakudate Lighting Architect&Associates

Photographs:
Katsuhisa Kida

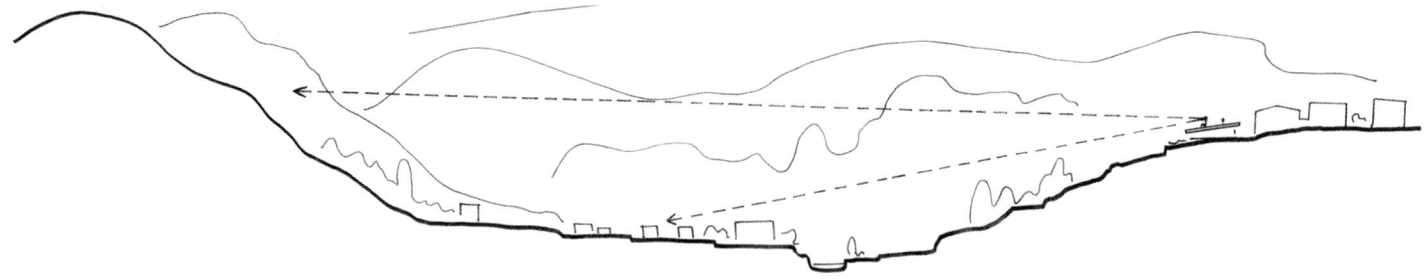

The living space extends onto the rooftop and merges with the exterior. With a freestanding wall to break the wind and provide privacy, the rooftop is equipped with a dining table, benches, a kitchen, a stove, and even a shower.

1. Skylights to keep the entrance hall bright
2. Mothers skylight to bring up the food from the kitchen
3. Roof-top shower
4. Roof-top kitchen
5. Fathers skylight to climb up from the main bed rooms
6. Older sister's skylight to climb up from the study room
7. Younger sister's skylight to climb up from children's room

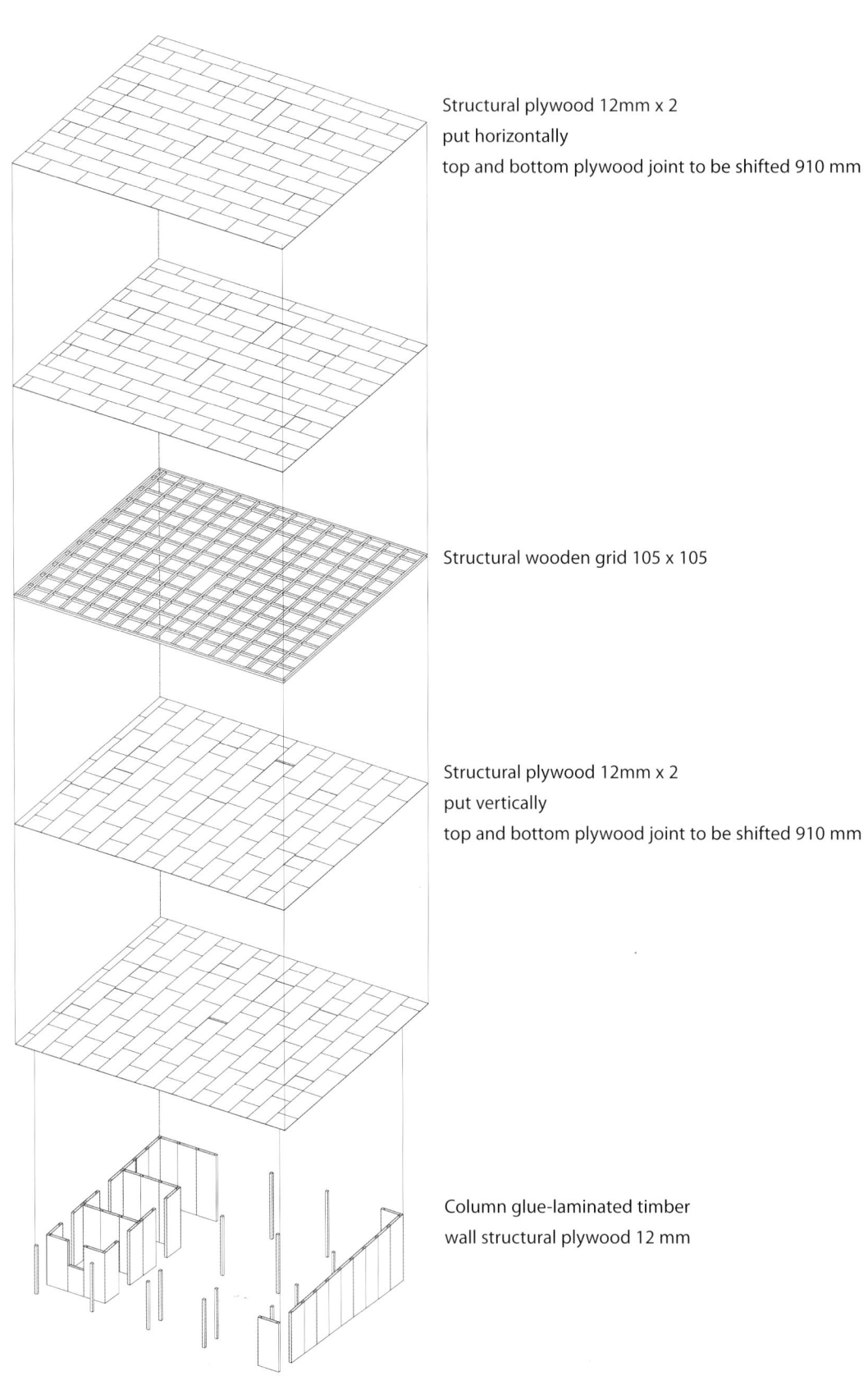

Ground floor plan
1. Entrance
2. Living room
3. Kitchen
4. Bathroom
5. Closet
6. Parent's bedroom
7. Study room
8. Children's bedroom
9. Closet

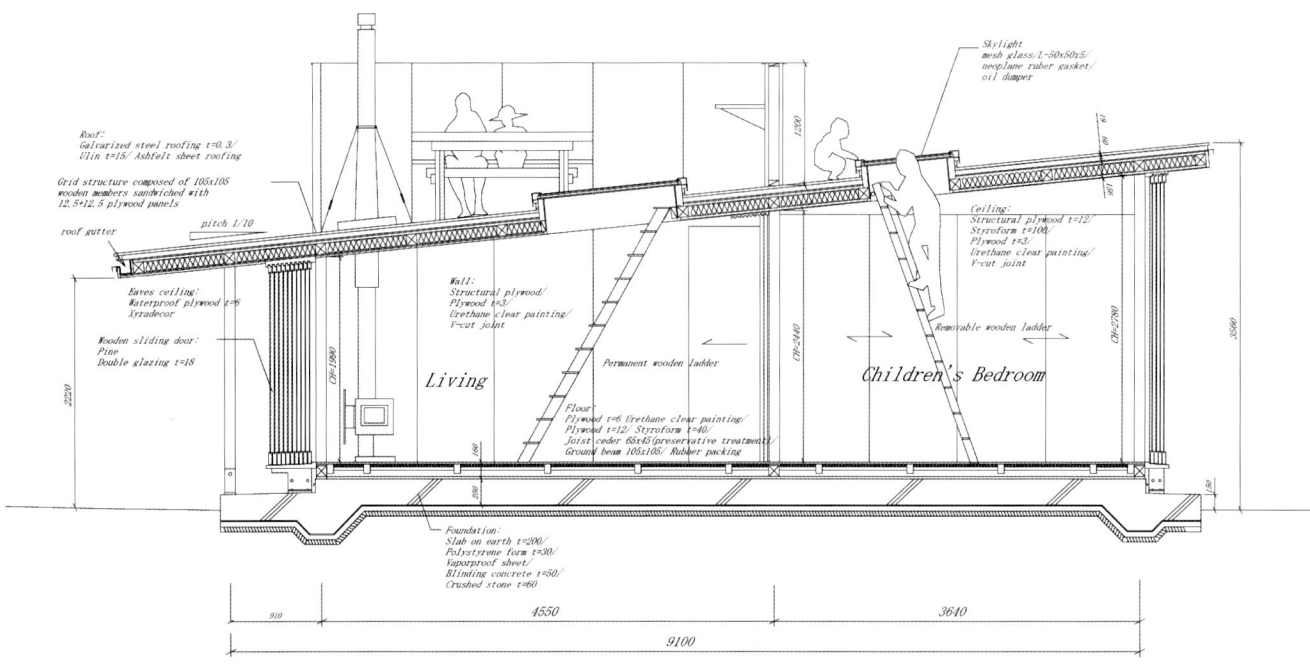

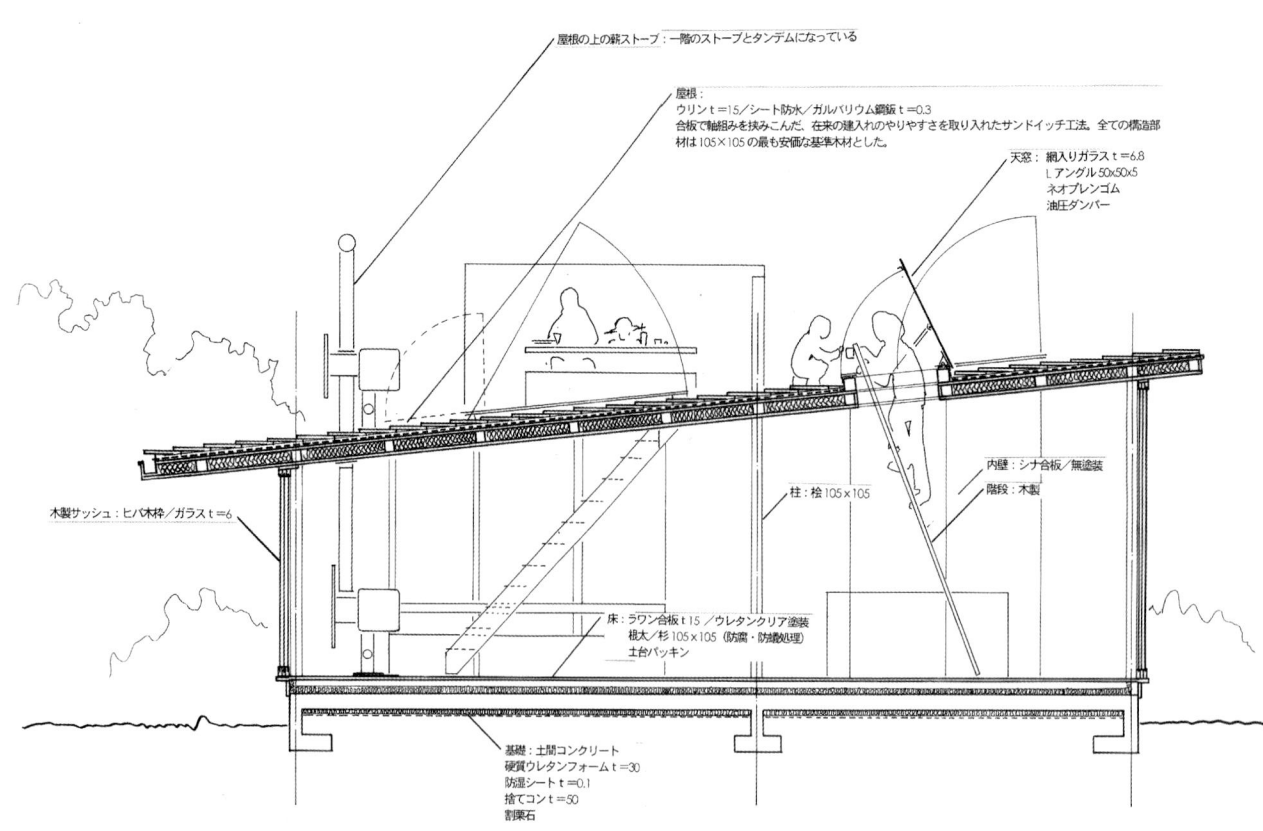

By maintaining a simple plan and utilizing a lightweight, yet earthquake responsive structure, the house provides a visually and tactilely generous space for the family. The thin roof, timber columns, and structural plywood panels allow for a flexible, partitioned space.

Tadao Ando

4 x 4 House

The site is a beachfront facing the Seto Inland Sea. On the opposite shore 4 kilometers away lies Hokudan-town on the Awaji Island, the epicenter of the 1995 Great Hanshin Earthquake. To the east stretches the Akashi strait Bridge. This location has presented the architect with the opportunity to develop the project by looking at the Awaji Island where he had been given the chance to work on various projects such as the Water Temple and Yumebutai, and at the Akashi Bridge, a demonstration of Japan's world-class construction technology.

The site is subject to erosion by the sea. A good part of the land has already turned into a sandy beach of rare beauty, leaving a mere patch of dry land behind the breakwater. The four-story tower has a square plan of 4m x 4m, whose uppermost level is a cube 4m on each side that protrudes towards the sea and that is shifted to the east side by one meter, thus saving the space for stairs. The landscape framed within this cube is a panorama sweeping over the Inland Sea, the Awaji Island and the Awaji Bridge where, for the client who makes a living in this region as well as for the architect, thoughts and memories of the earthquake are embedded. The ground floor accommodates the entrance, bathroom, and lavatory; the second floor the bedroom; the third floor the study, the fourth floor the living room and kitchen.

After the completion of the house a man who had occasionally visited it rented the adjacent land from the owner of the 4 x 4 house and asked the architect to design him a house. The architect is now considering the possibility of building a house symmetrical to the previous one but made of wood instead of concrete. In the near future, the two houses of "similar shape yet different materials" will sit side by side facing the Inland Sea.

Location:
Kobe, Hyogo, Japan

Photographs:
Mitsuo Matsuoka

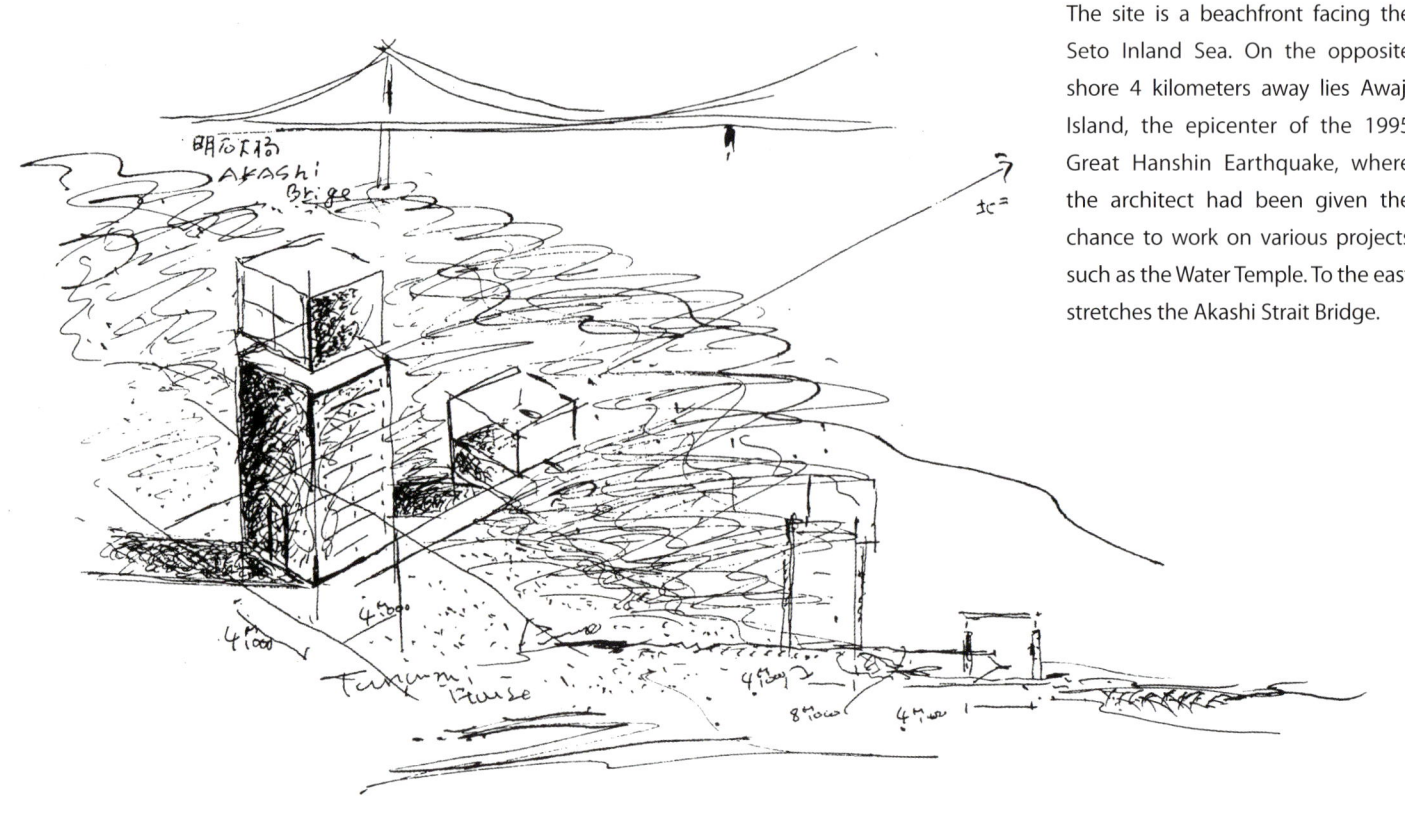

The site is a beachfront facing the Seto Inland Sea. On the opposite shore 4 kilometers away lies Awaji Island, the epicenter of the 1995 Great Hanshin Earthquake, where the architect had been given the chance to work on various projects such as the Water Temple. To the east stretches the Akashi Strait Bridge.

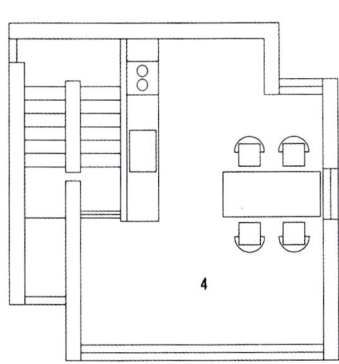
4th floor - living room

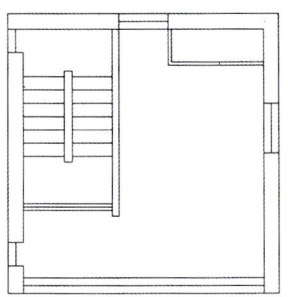
3rd floor - study room

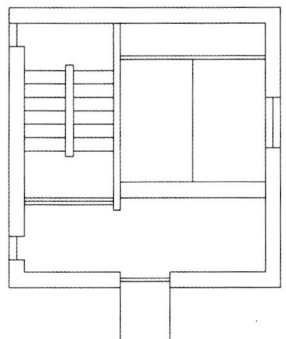
2nd floor – bedroom

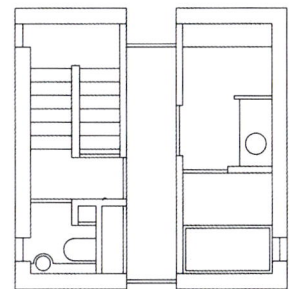
Ground floor - bathroom

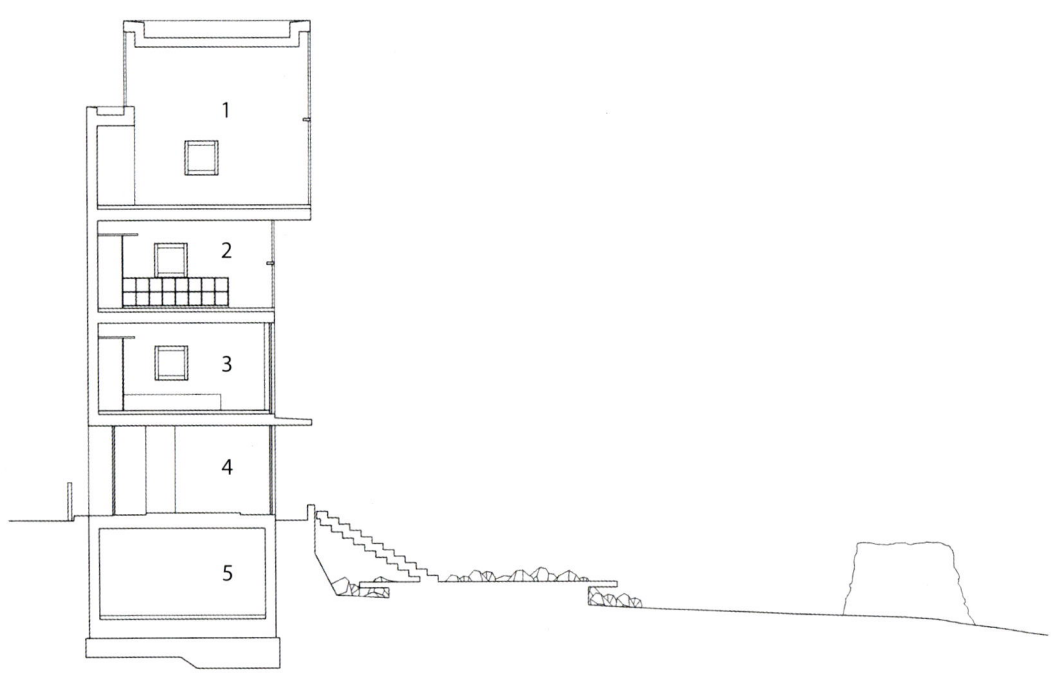

Section
1. Living room
2. Study room
3. Bedroom
4. Entrance
5. Storage

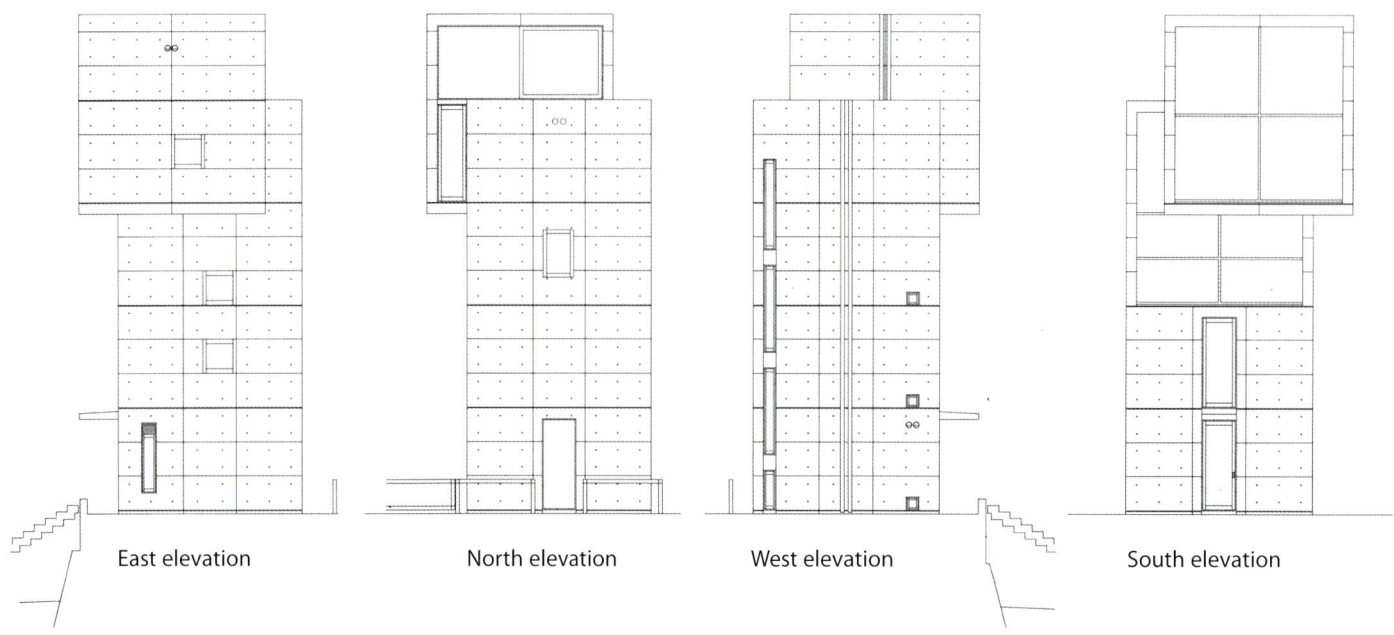

East elevation North elevation West elevation South elevation

118

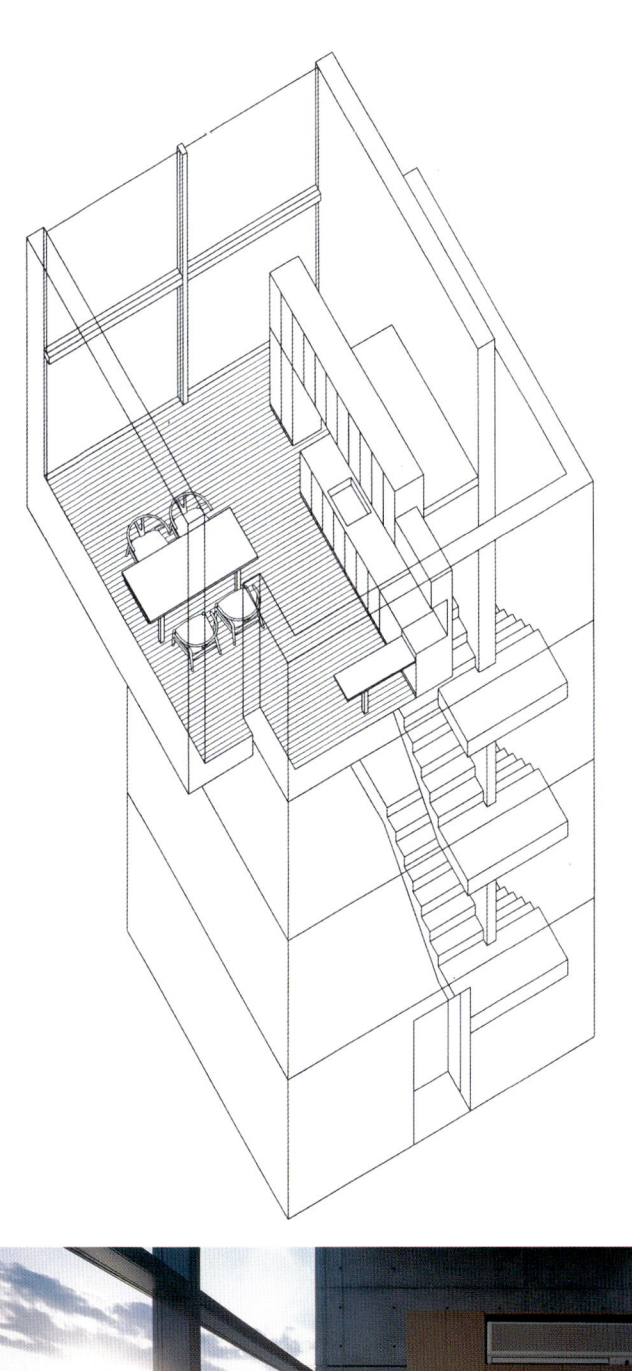

119

Crosson Clarke Carnachan Architects

Coromandel Bach

This mid-sized house (with 128 sqm of floor space) was conceived as a container sitting lightly on the land for habitation or the dream of habitation. The intention was to reinterpret the New Zealand building tradition of the crafting of wood - the expression of structure, cladding, lining and joinery in a raw and unique way. The construction is reminiscent of the 'trip' or 'rafter' dams common in the Coromandel region at the turn of last century: heavy vertical structural members supporting horizontal boarding.

The unadorned natural timber, a sustainable and renewable resource, provides a connection to nature and the natural. A simple mechanism to the deck allows the 'box' to open up on arrival, providing a stage for living, and to close down on departure, providing protection.

The house has a simple rectangular plan that sits across the contour in a patch of cleared bush in the manner of the rural shed, facing north and enjoying unobstructed views.

The living room is open to the outside and the sun, a metaphorical tent or campsite, while the bunkrooms are enclosed and cool. The large fireplace allows winter occupation and the open bathroom and moveable bath allows the rituals of showering and bathing to become an experience connected to nature.

This 'bach' is an attempt to provide an environment to capture the essential spirit of a New Zealand vacation home set in the scenic New Zealand landscape. ('Bach' is a typical New Zealand word that describes a weekend cottage or house, usually at the beach).

Location:
Coromandel, New Zealand
Photographs:
Patrick Reynolds

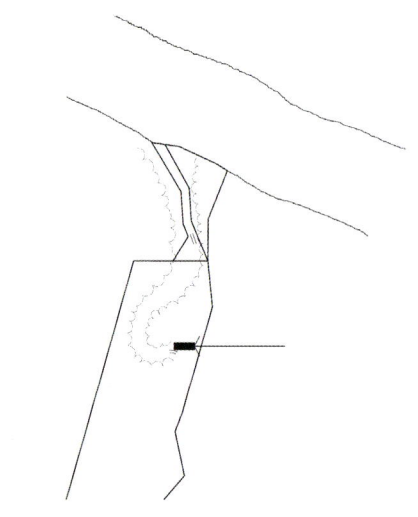

Site plan

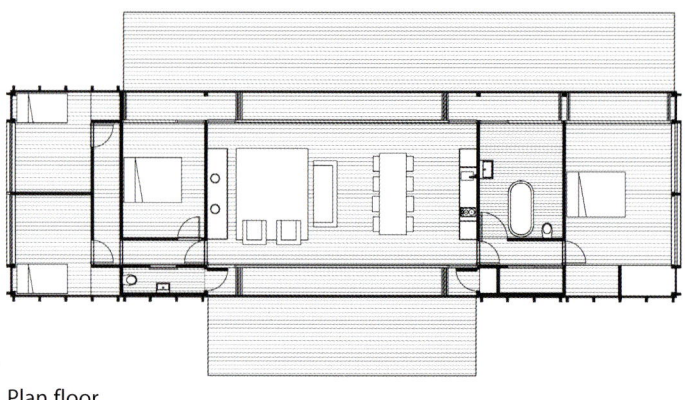

Plan floor

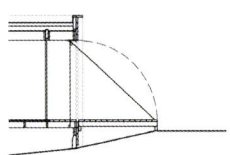

Section - Deck lowered

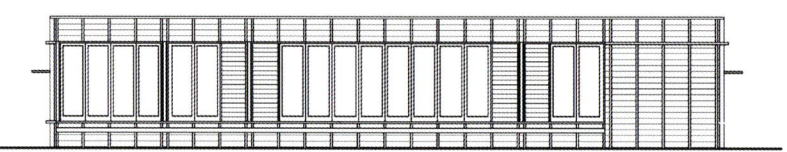

North elevation

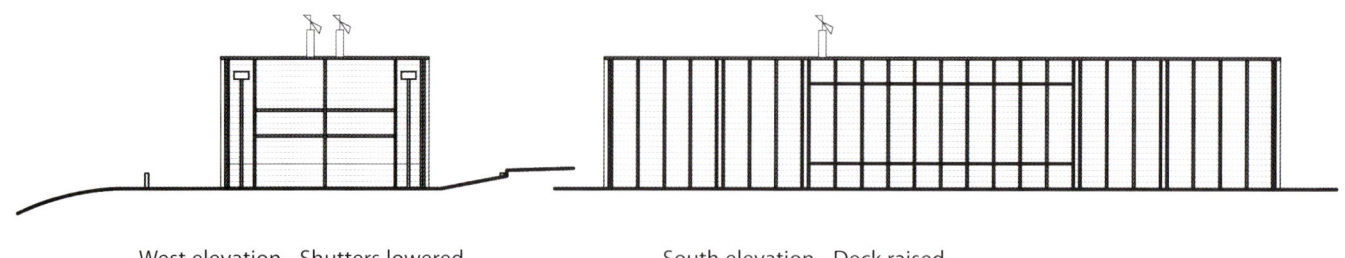

West elevation - Shutters lowered

South elevation - Deck raised

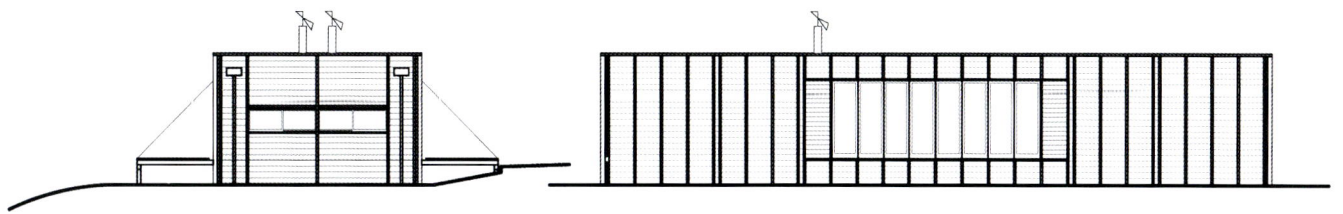

West elevation - Shutters raised

South elevation - Deck lowered

127

Cross-section

1. Flashing
2. Lawson Cyprus cladding/decking
3. Building wrap
4. Insulation
5. Membrane roof over plywood
6. Steel beam / lintel
7. Exposed Lawson Cyprus rafters
8. Plywood ceiling
9. Timber flooring
10. Timber joists
11. Timber piles / bearers
12. Bi-fold doors
13. Single block
14. Spectra rope
15. 20mm Stainless steel hinge
16. Electric motor
17. Axle
18. River stones

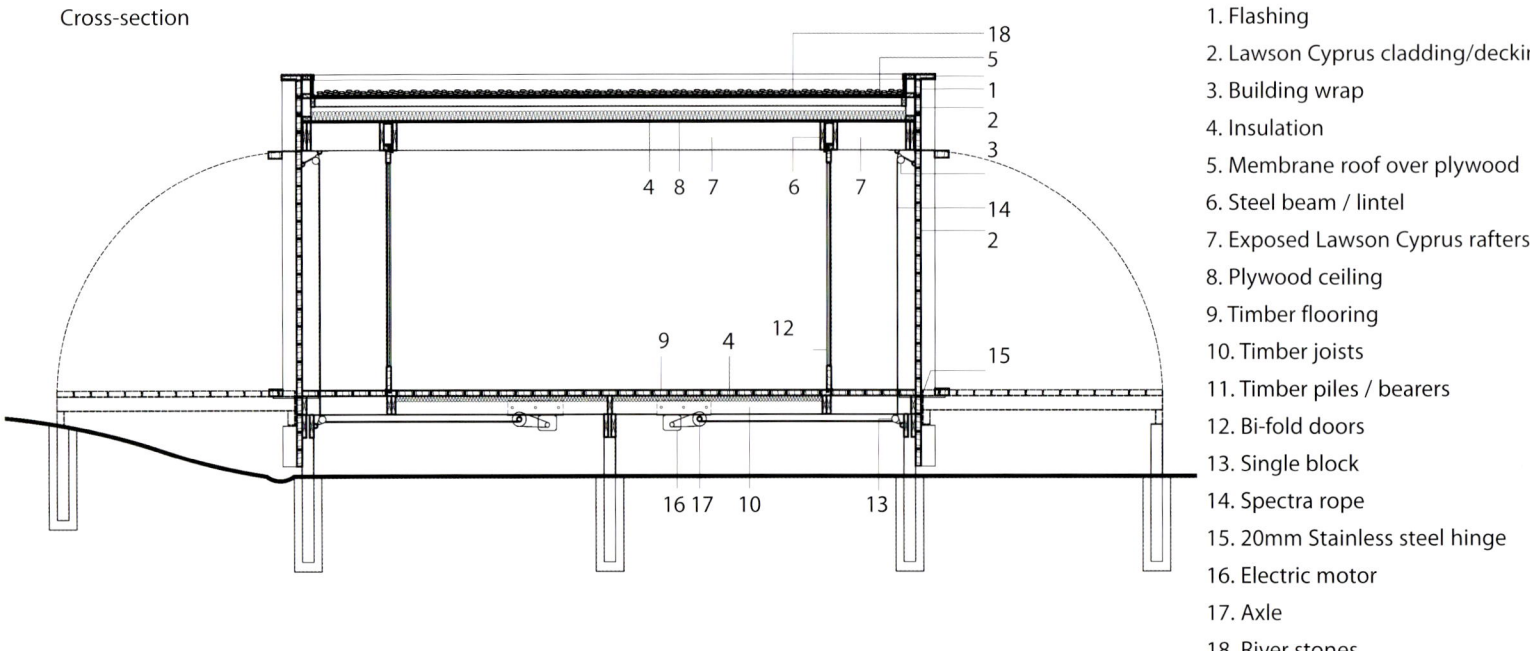

The living room is open to the outside and the sun, like a tent or campsite. The open bathroom and moveable bath allows the rituals of showering and bathing to become an experience connected to nature.

KHR AS Arkitekter

Guesthouse at Nissum Bredning

In the late 1930's, painter Jens Søndergaard moved into a house in Toftum, and in a letter to his friend, Leo Svane he described "landscapes so wonderfully expansive they were beyond comparison with Thy".
The artist's fascination with the special light, the strong sweeping Toftum Bjerge hills and the Limfjord region's wide open skies inspired a number of distinctive paintings, often done in the same area where the guest house was built. The house is built into a hilly slope, with a 200 degree panorama view from east to west over an open, un-built dune and meadow area running down toward the Nissum Bredning coast.

One of the goals was to capture the light from the sky in a continuous spatial sequence in one building, which, when seen from any direction, respects the profile of the hill ridge. The guest area consists of two parts, a concrete slab covered with basalt, and a copper shell. The slab serves as the floor, a continuous plane running from the morning terrace in the east to the evening terrace in the west. The shell serves as both facade and roof and is closed toward the slope to the south and open toward the north.

The roof is punctured by a continuous skylight, which spatially separates the secondary functions in the closed core toward the south from the primary functions in the more open spatial sequence in the other three directions. The bearing construction consists of steel frames, while the roof and outer walls consist of prefabricated wooden coffers dimensioned according to the building's primary grid.

The exterior copper siding is a rare sight in Denmark; felt with a thin, flexible copper covering, with a textured, waffled surface due to the compression of the copper and felt.

Location:
Jutland, Denmark

Photographs:
Ib Sorensen

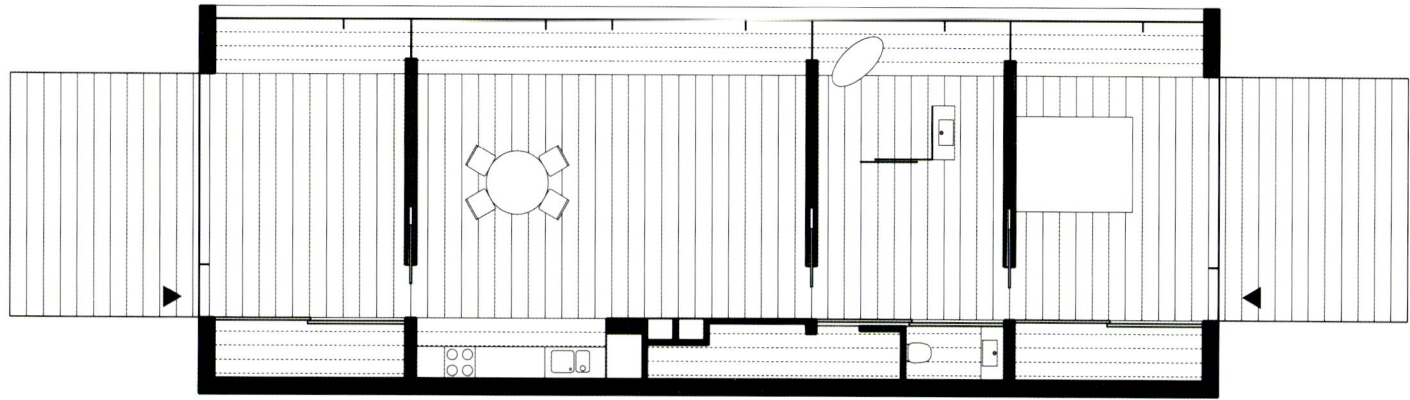

mae architects

m - house

The m-house project started life in a slightly different form to the mass produced product shown in the majority of the accompanying photographs and drawings. Early in 2003 the client, Tim Pyne approached the architect to design him a weekend home to be set on a plot of land overlooking a wetland estuary in Essex. The sensitivities of the surrounding area meant that permission could only be gained to place two leisure caravans (non-permanent structures) on the site. The client wanted a weekend home that would possess the build, space and design qualities of a contemporary London apartment.

The first task was to research the legal description of a leisure caravan, in order to ascertain the design parameters of the project. The results of this research produced some startling results, firstly that the laws describing this form of accommodation are amazingly simple, because no one had bothered to push the form's possibilities since the late 1940's. Basically a caravan is an accommodation unit that must come to site in no more then two sections, which must be towed into place. These two sections must be fixed together mechanically in order to complete the structure. The dimensional requirements of the structure are defined by the internal or net dimensions. The internal dimensions of 18.2m by 6m gave a generous plan of up to 109.2 sqm with a maximum internal height of 3m; this seemed to offer great possibilities for the project.

The design of the two caravan units, which were to be placed end to end forming one building was governed by the client's wish to have the maximum possible visual and physical connection with the surrounding landscape. One unit was to house living spaces, the other bedroom and bathroom spaces. Each unit would take the form of an off site manufactured, elegant stressed-skin ply structure, (engineered by Techniker). Simple additions of built-in furniture forming kitchen and bathrooms would maintain the open aspect of the interior, which because of the nature of the lining material was taking on the characteristics of a cabin or train carriage.

Excited by the potential of the project the client decided that the scheme should be re-designed as a single unit that could be retailed. He had decided to start a company with the intension of producing units of this type which could take advantage of the off site manufacturing potential and eased planning restrictions which the design delivered. The architects were asked to produce a rationalized scheme for mass production, which eliminated some of the idiosyncrasies of the one off weekend home project. They produced a robust steel frame solution which had the advantage of being crane deliverable.

The plan is set out with a large kitchen dining area, bathroom, WC, washing room and two cabin-like bedrooms. The interior maintained its timber-lined character, with homely inclusions such as the timber-burning stove, which are augmented with under floor heating through out. The external weathering is achieved in the prototype with profiled aluminum rain cladding and other material treatments such as timber or terracotta depending on site requirements.

Location:
Essex, UK

Photographs:
Morley von Sternberg

The beauty of this building type is that it deals with so many pertinent issues such as affordability, factory production, and the imperative for environmental sustainability. It can sit lightly on green-field sites without causing permanent damage; and allows for the separation of building costs from land costs and so cuts out one of the key cost restrictions to housing.

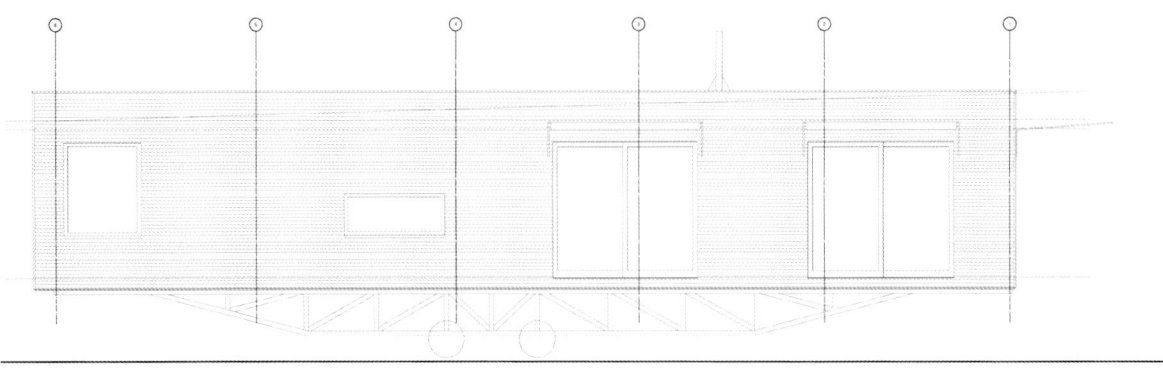

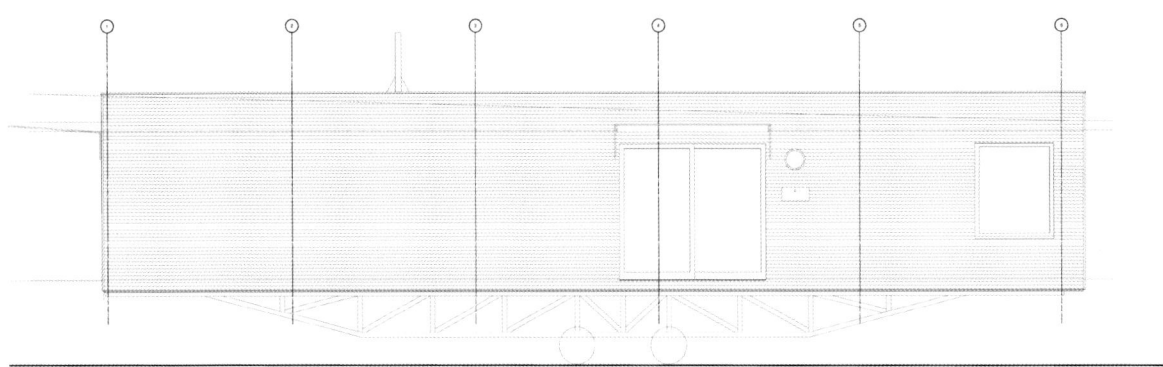

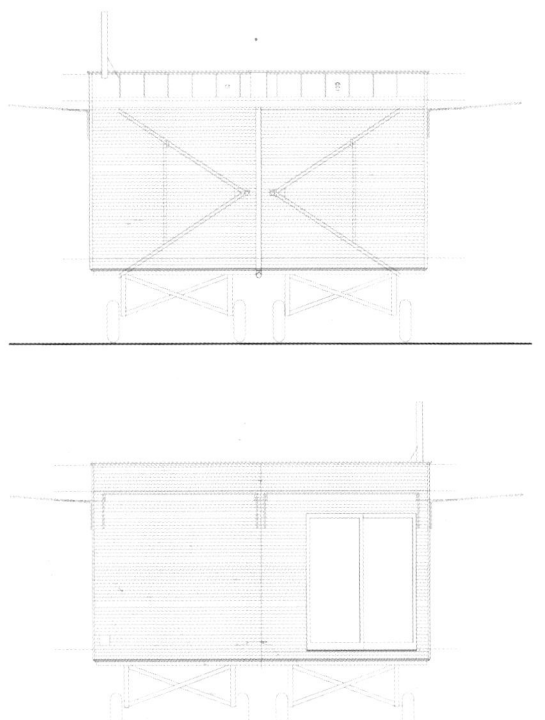

Elevations

Plan

1. External timber ramp
2. Entrance
3. Living area
4. Boiler and washroom
5. Bed 1
6. Bed 2
7. Bathroom
8. W.C
9. External timber deck

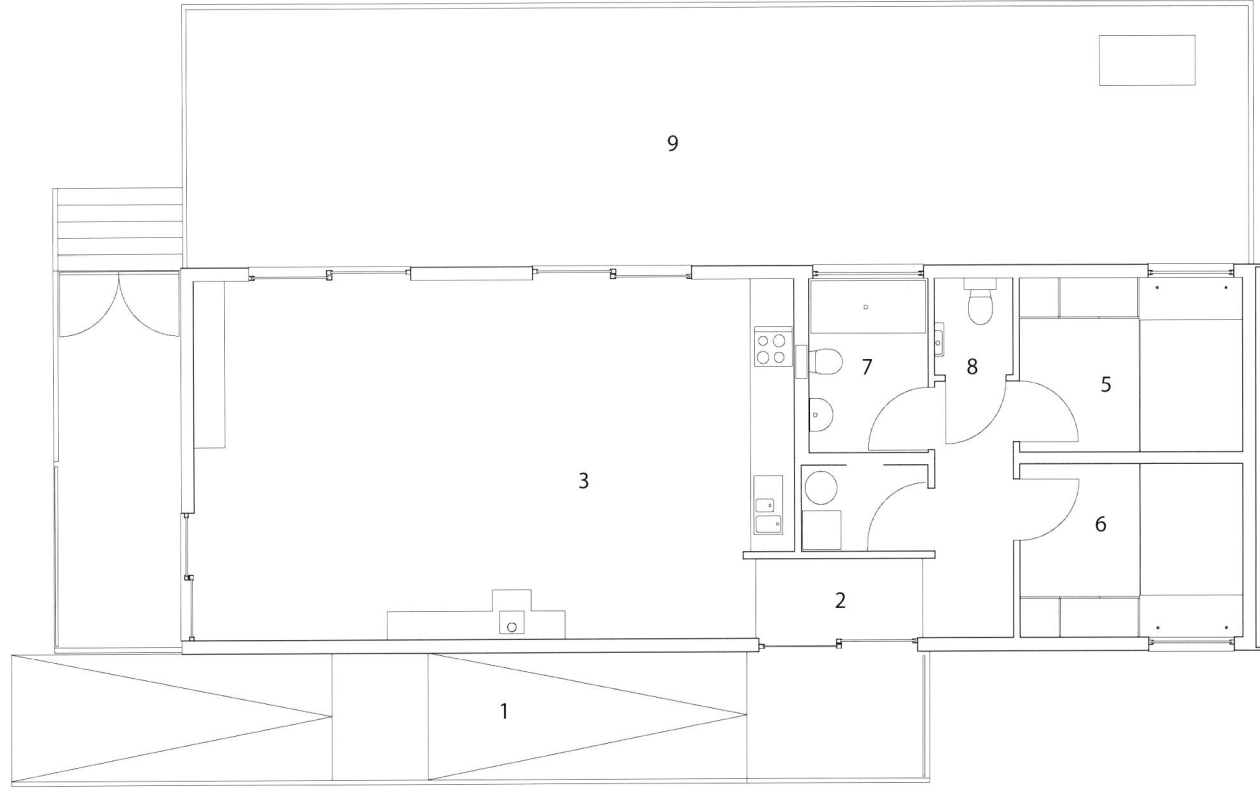

Alberto Campo Baeza

De Blas House

This house is, above all, the architect's response to the site, which is located on the top of a hill looking north towards the mountains near Madrid.

The design addresses both the mountain and the distant views by integrating two volumes, one more earthy and designed for living, the other airy and fragile, meant for contemplating the natural surroundings and enjoying the views.

The first volume was built as a concrete box, which also became the platform and acted as a podium. Over this, the architect placed a transparent glass box, delicately covered with a precise steel structure painted white.

The concrete box, rooted in the ground like a cave, contains the living areas. The layout is clear and simple, with service areas in a row towards the back, and the spaces they serve placed towards the front of the house.

Stairs lead from this lower level to the glass box above the platform, which consists of an outdoor area and covered lookout, like a hut, with views to the mountain.

Light was a central concept in the design, continuing the tension between the two sections. In the upper part of the house, the architect worked with horizontal light crossing the horizontal space, and the ideas of transparency and continuous space. Standing in the shaded lookout, the observer can contemplate the mountain landscape, which is illuminated by the sun and emphasized, so that it seems to come towards him or her.

In the lower section, the enclosed space frames the light and the framed mountain landscape appears to flee away from the observer.

The house is an attempt towards a literal translation of the idea of a tectonic box placed over a stereotomic box. A process of distillation in order to arrive at what is essential in architecture. Once again, "more with less".

Location:
Madrid, Spain

Photographs:
Hisao Suzuki

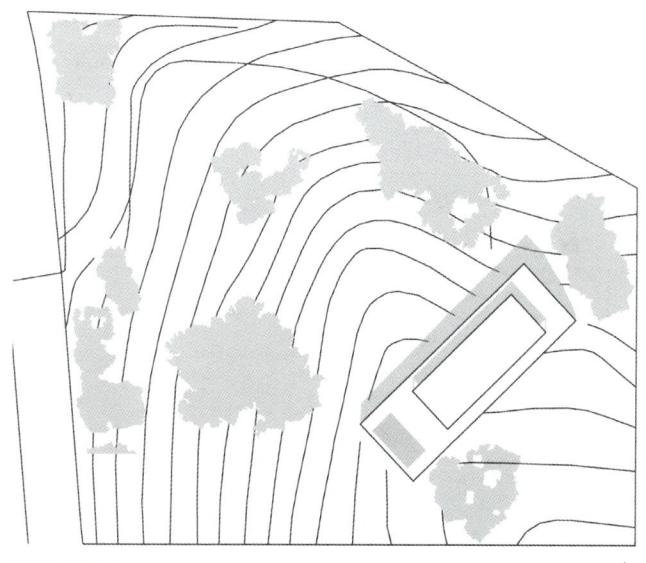

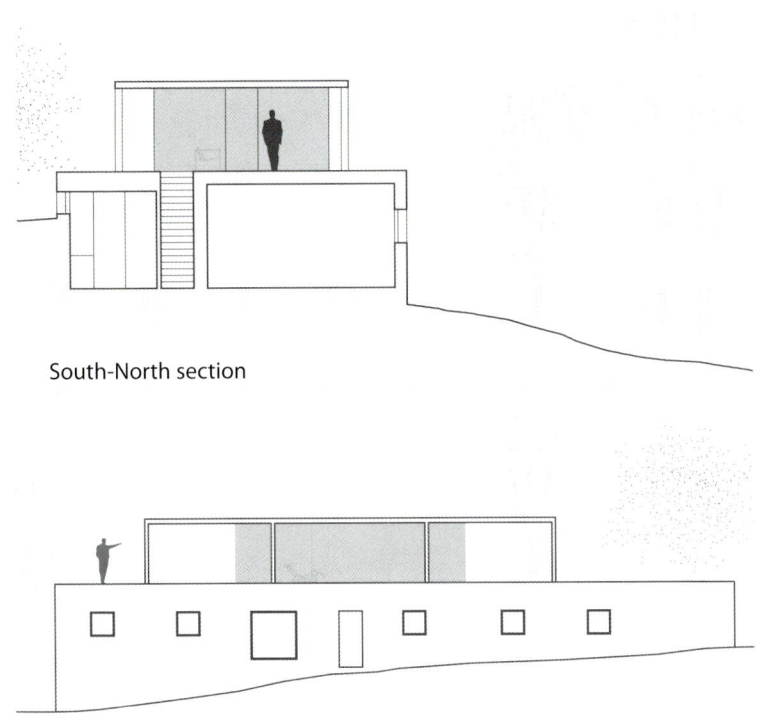

South-North section

North elevation

The base is a cave-like space that provides refuge. Above, a glass hut provides a space for contemplating nature. The measurements are exact and the proportions carefully calculated, creating a feeling of purity and peace.

The simple interiors in the lower volume frame the view and keep it separate, while in the upper section the glass walls make the house appear to be part of the landscape itself.

1. 5 + 5 fixed Stadip glazing
2. 84 x 226 cm folding door with 10 mm safety glass
3. Continuous concrete, waterproof finish
4. Sloped damp-resistant concrete compression layer
5. Separating layer
6. 3 cm extruded polystyrene insulation
7. Waterproof membrane
8. Separating layer
9. 5 cm compression layer
10. Drop ceiling
11. 0.5% slope
12. 80x210 cm folding door with 10 mm safety glass
13. 12 mm double panel of pladur/plaster painted white
14. High-density polyurethane foam insulation
15. 25 cm thick reinforced concrete wall
16. 60x40x3 cm stone paving
17. Bond coat (2 cm).
18. Bed of sand (3 cm).
19. Compression layer (3 cm).
20. PVC.
21. "Isover" insulation (4 cm).
22. Compression layer (5 cm).
23. 20x120 cm Macrofur
24. Wall of perforated brick
25. Reinforced concrete bolster
26. H-50 concrete
27. Profile finishing
28. Reinforced concrete beam
29. Fastening strip
30. 12 mm double panel of pladur/plaster painted white
31. Step with 3 cm stone
32. 7 cm stone skirting board
33. Natural ground
34. 1-2 mm "Rhenofol CV" waterproofing
35. Fiber glass felt protection
36. Polystyrene Roofmate SL insulation, 1250x600x30mm
37. 0.25 polyethylene "Rhenofol PE" barrier
38. HEB 180 profile painted white
39. Perimeter finish, Roofmate
40. HEB 180 profile painted white
41. Check throat
42. 15x120 cm Macrufor
43. 14 mm finish
44. 4x1.4 cm fastening
45. Metal pillar painted white
46. 5 + 5 fixed Stadip glazing
47. 20x20 cm anchor plate
48. Continuous concrete, waterproof finish
49. 20x120 cm Macrufor plate
50. High-density polyurethane foam insulation
51. 12 mm double panel of pladur/plaster painted white
52. PVC check throat
53. 180x180 window with double glazing and aluminum carpentry
54. 0.5 % slope
55. 25 cm thick reinforced concrete wall

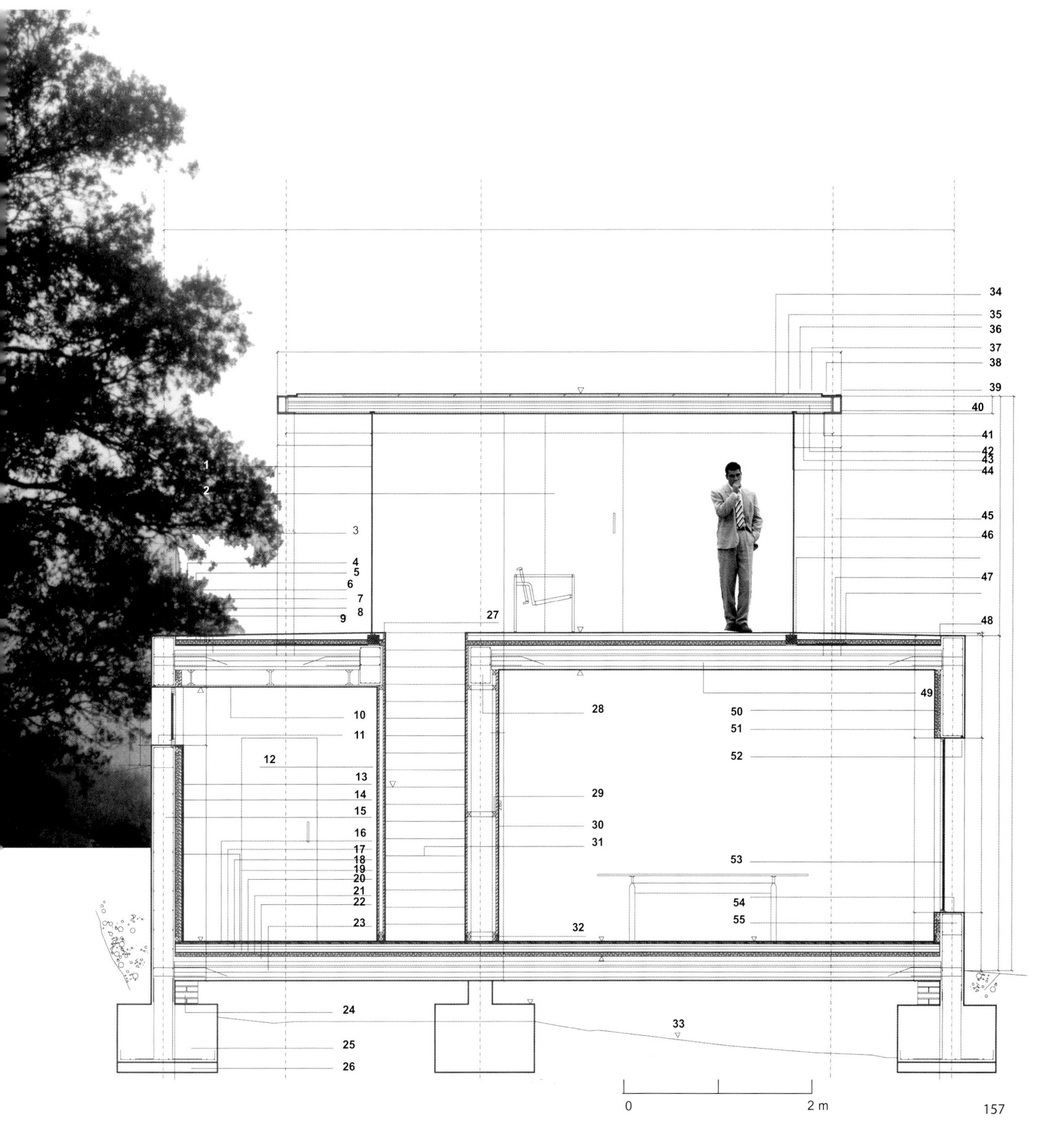

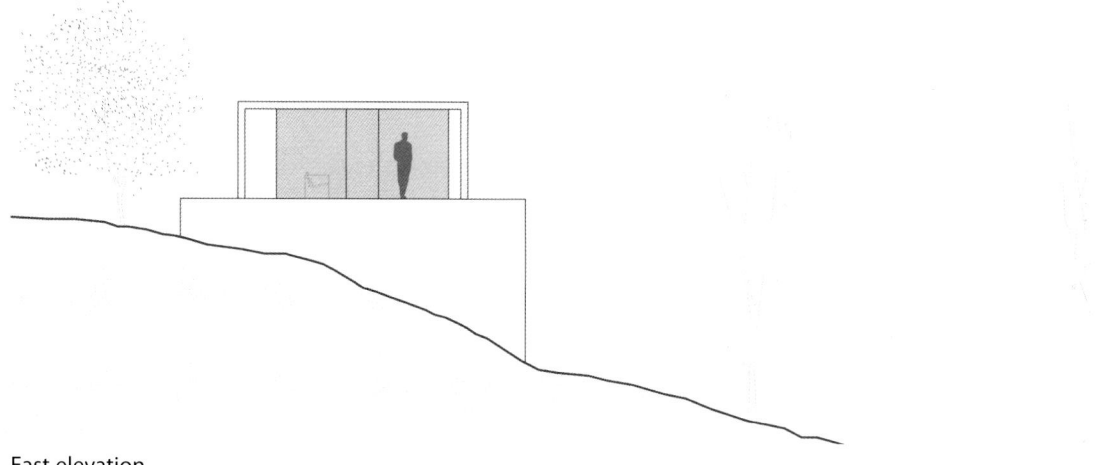

East elevation

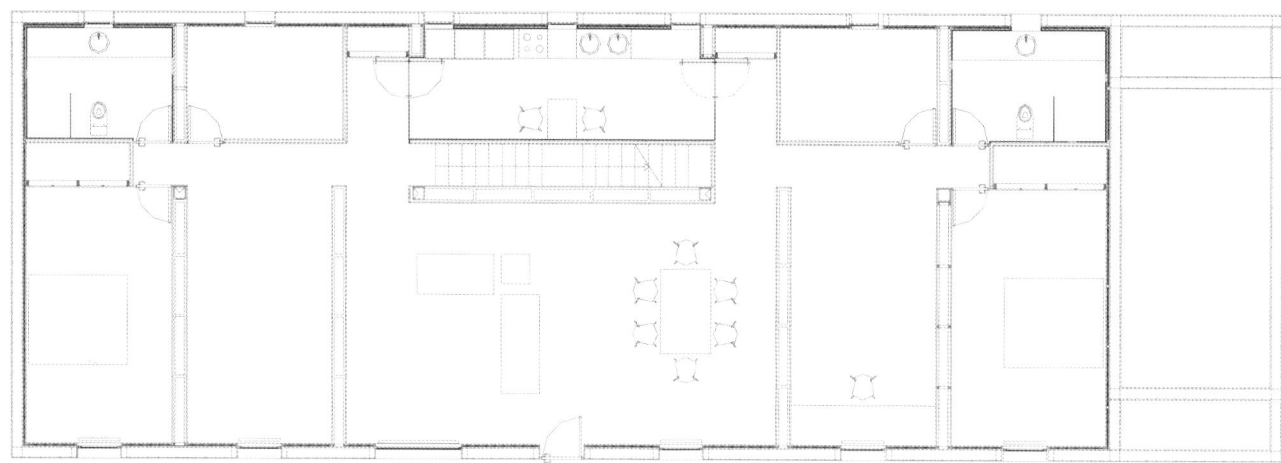

Ground floor plan

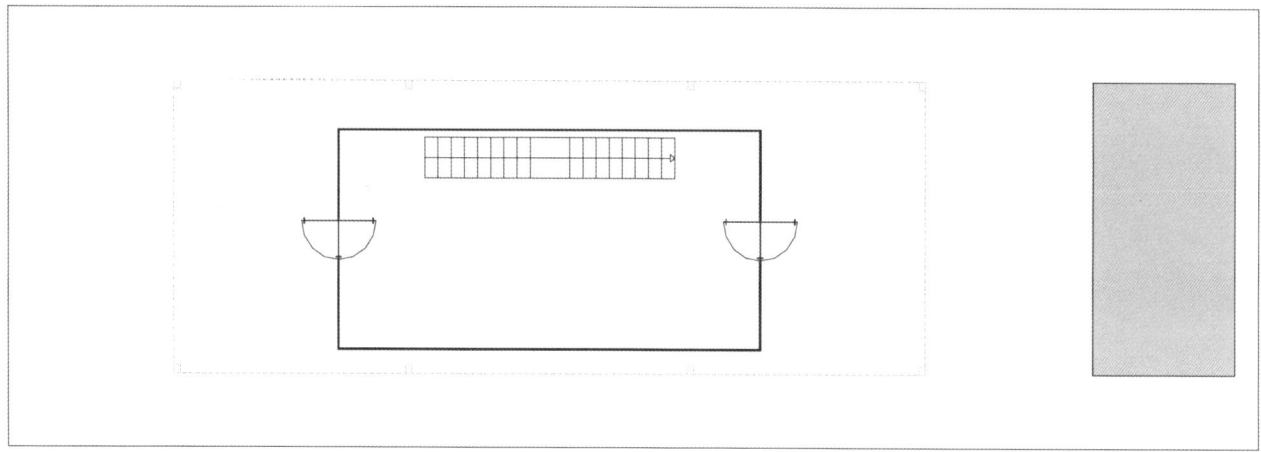

Podium

Huttunen & Lipasti

Villa Linnanmäki

The villa is located on a narrow strip of woodland that separates the open agricultural terrain from a lake; it consists in a dwelling unit of modest size and a separate sauna cabin. These constructions are sited on opposite sides of a pathway that winds its way through a group of birch trees that brighten the more solemn context of pine forests. The path comes down from the edge of the field, passes between the house and the sauna cabin and continues to the lakeshore. The house offers a generous open façade towards the lake, as opposed to the other three sides, that are almost blank, facing the woodland and the fields.

All the walls are sided with the plentiful local pine wood. The traditional protective black oil finish of the timber buildings replicates the dark tones of the edge of the forest. The open lakeside façade reveals the warm golden tones of the same timber showing its natural color, which predominates throughout the interiors as well as the terrace-deck that extends a few yards in front of the house. This functions as a welcome addition to the living room, which is relatively compact. Immediately in front of the house, the birch trees shelter the building's open front from the excessive sun, and the foliage repeats the honey tones of the interior walls; otherwise the plot has been left in its natural state, an untouched context that the buildings are inscribed upon with candid frankness. The interior space is divided by a masonry wall, around which the water system has been centered, together with the heating appliance, a wood-burning storage heater. The façades of the upper floor module have been sided with the same metal sheeting as the roof, integrating the volume into the lower floor and maintaining the proximity to the ground that characterizes the buildings when they are approached from the rear. Seen from the front, the upper floor has a totally different geometry, only the golden interior, which glows from the balcony towards the lake, reveals the identity of the two bodies. This space contains the master bedroom, which overlooks the surrounding landscape from a slight vantage point.

Location:
Somerniemi, Finland
Photographs:
Marko Huttunen

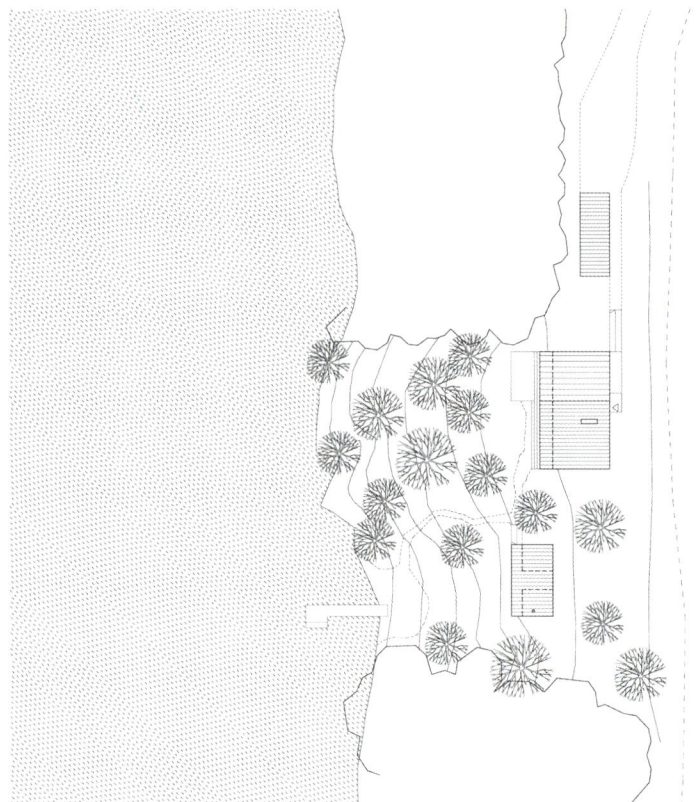

Site plan

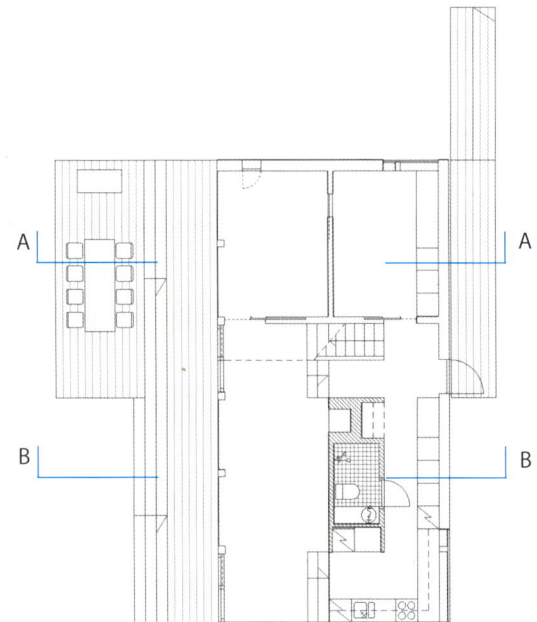

House - Ground floor

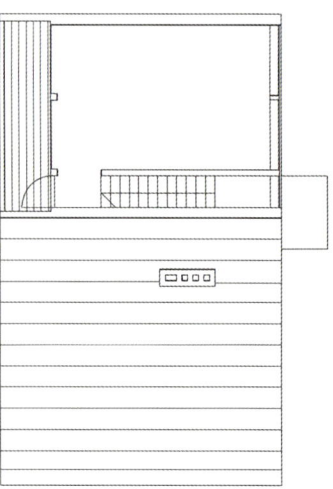

House - First floor

162

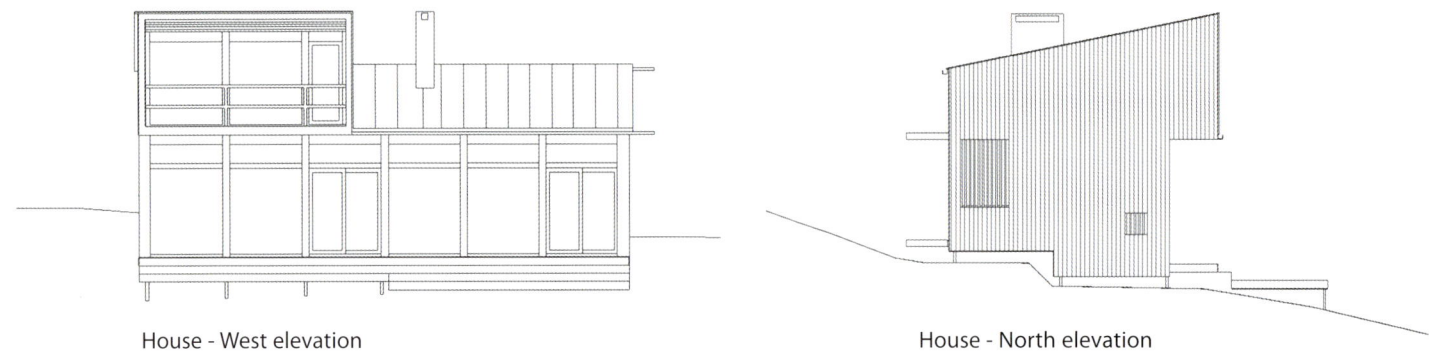

House - West elevation

House - North elevation

164

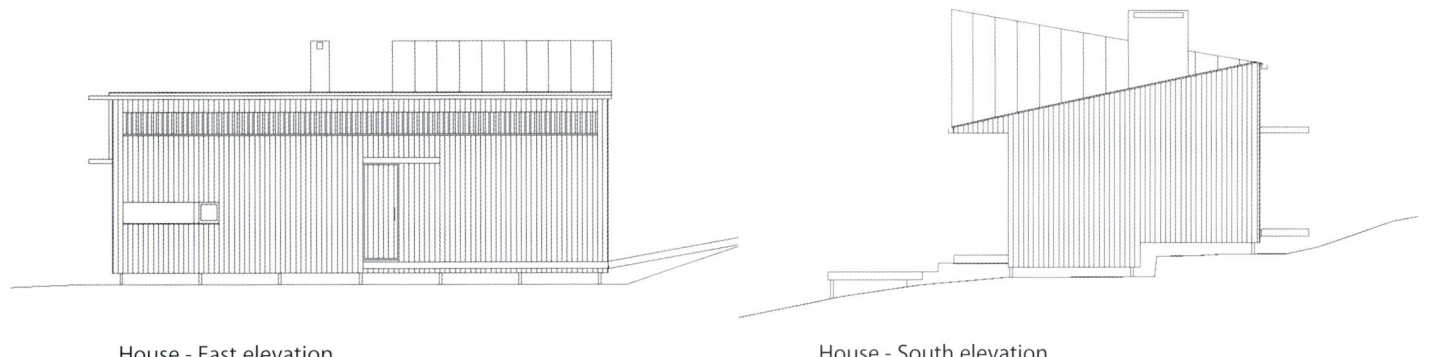

House - East elevation

House - South elevation

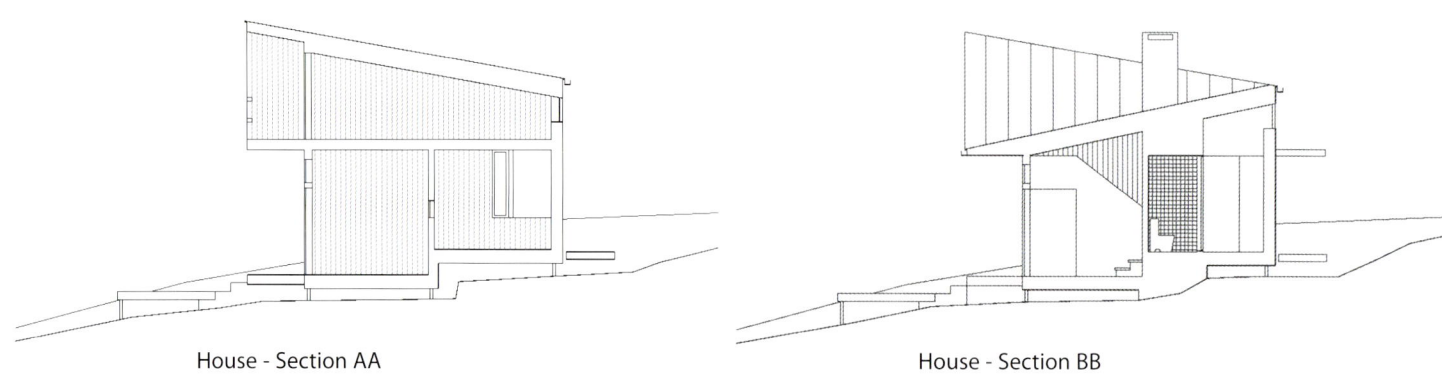

House - Section AA House - Section BB

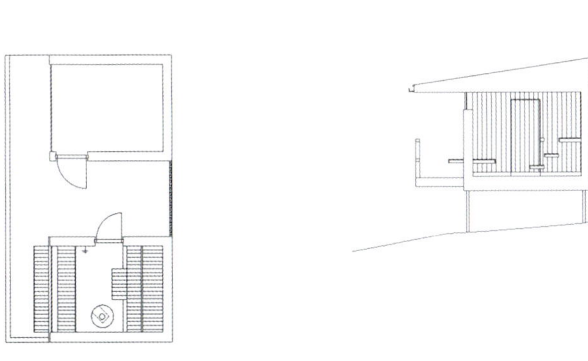

Sauna - Plan   Sauna - Section

169

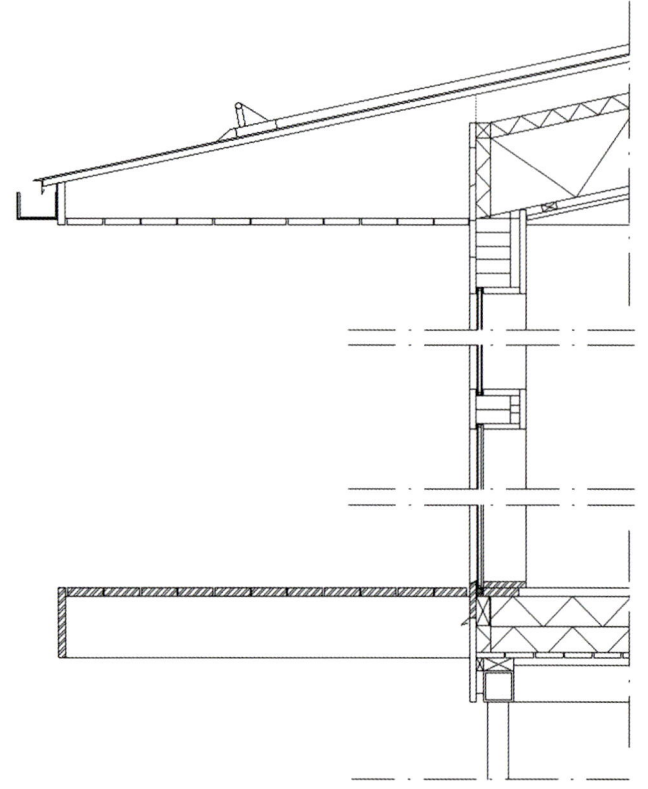
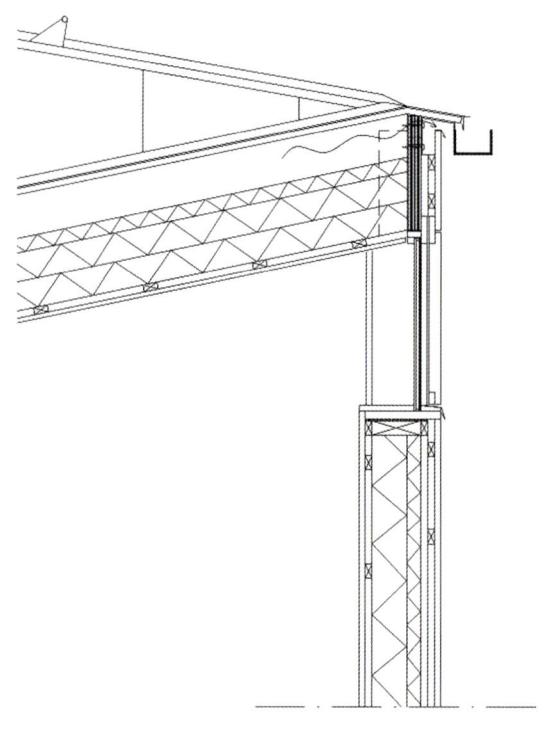

Koh Kitayama + architecture WORKSHOP

TN House

The client's requirements were simple: the first floor was to be designed so as to be converted into a gallery in the future, and a balcony for drinking tea was also to be created. However, the project proved difficult. The site was only about 53 sqm in area, the budget was limited, and the ground was surprisingly weak.

The end result is a symmetrical floor plan, with the structure and technical services concentrated in a central core, at the top of which is the balcony. This arrangement partially eliminates the problem of future differential layout, without resorting to the use of piles.

The structure itself is lightweight (out of necessity, due to the earth's weak composition), comprised of a wood frame strengthened only where necessary with light steel work.

Everything is a tight fit in this house. During the design process the architects had initially tried to persuade the clients that the inclusion of a balcony was a bad idea. However, they now concede that it is this balcony that ultimately enriches the house.

The finishing materials are as pared down as the design, with plywood and cement board used abundantly.

Location:
Yokohama, Kanagawa Prefecture, Japan

Photographs:
Nobuaki Nakagawa

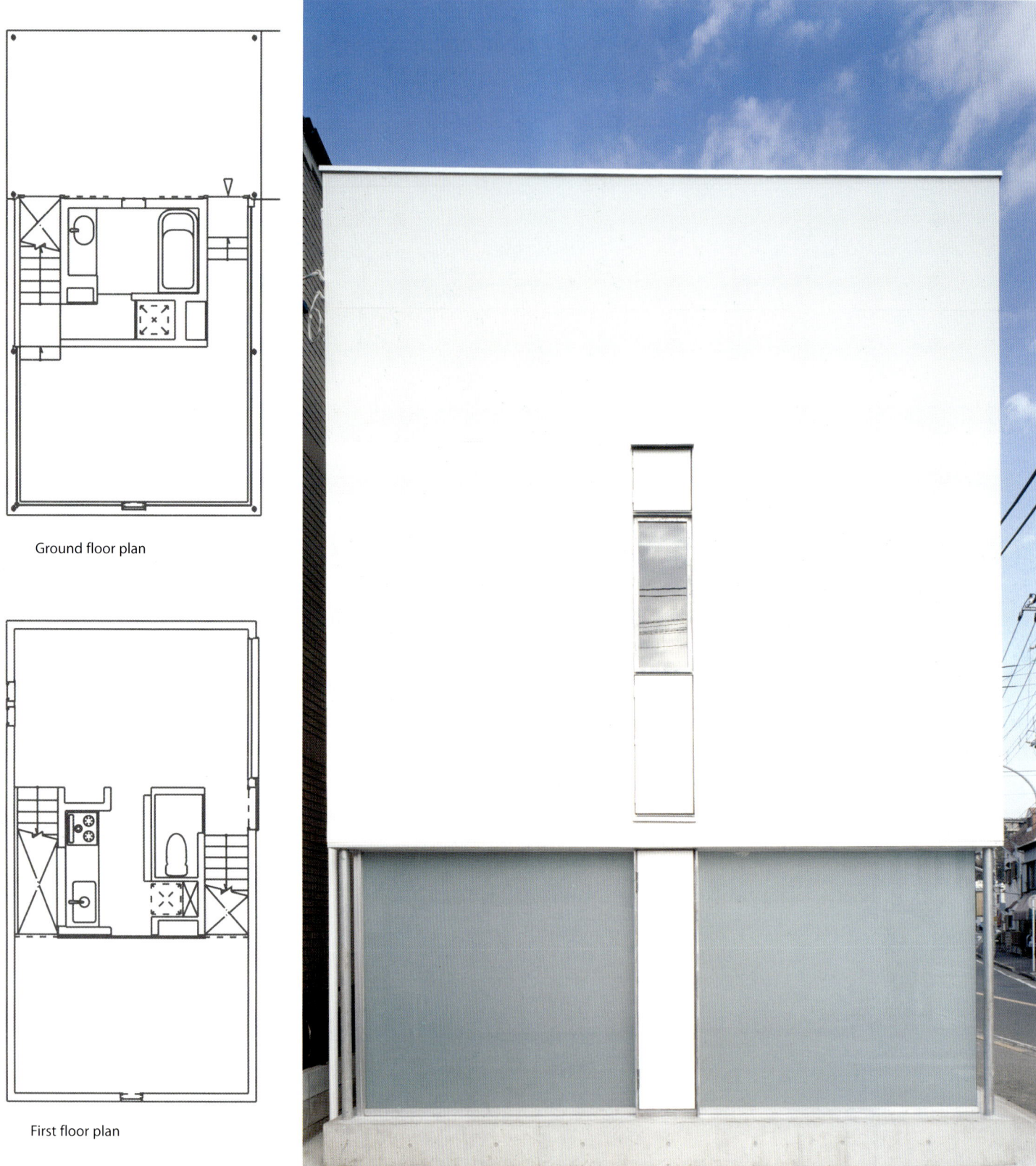

Ground floor plan

First floor plan

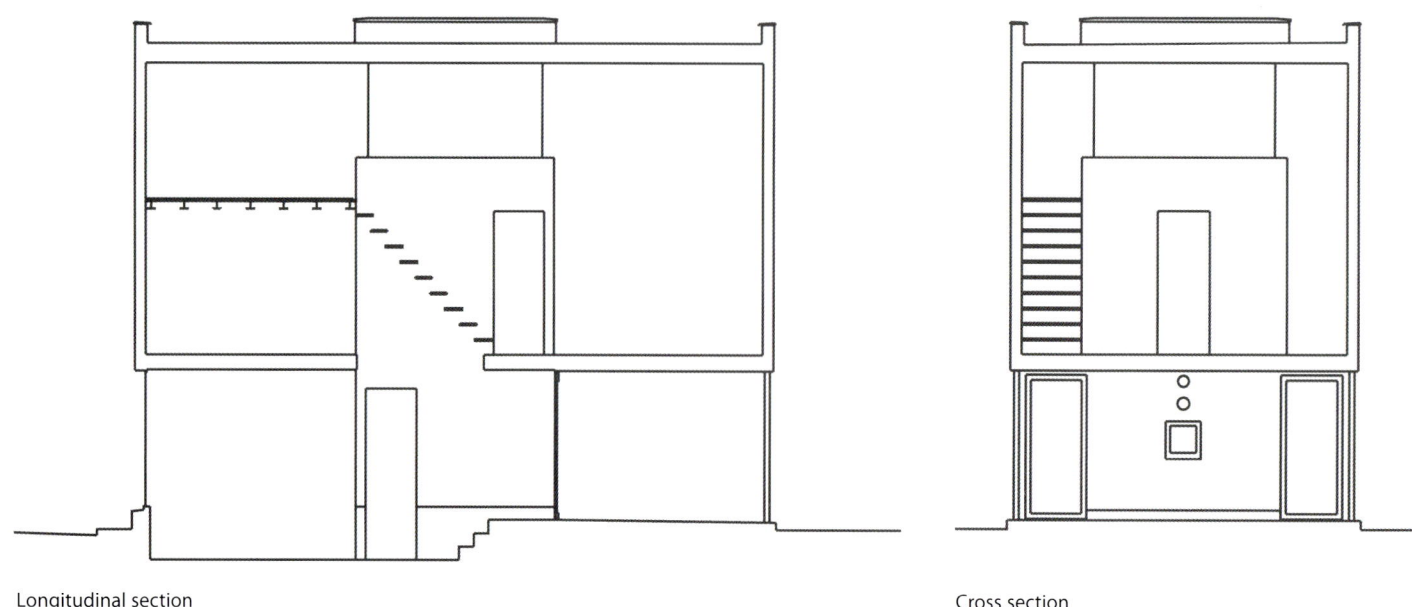

Longitudinal section

Cross section

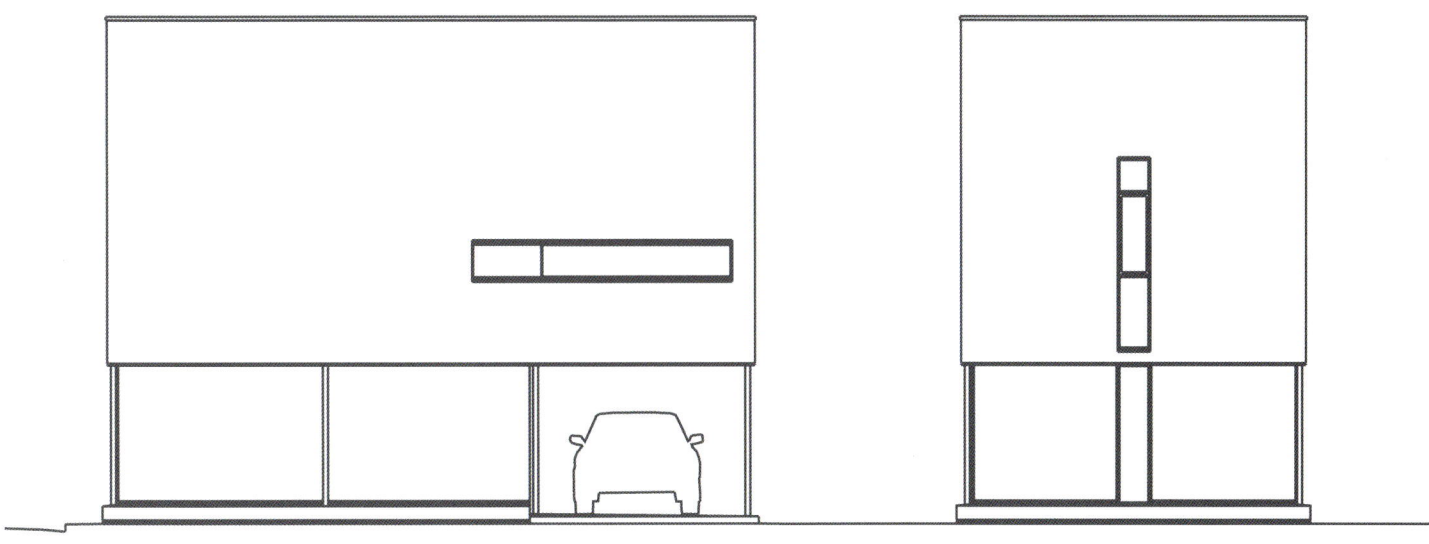

Side elevation	Front elevation

The end result is a symmetrical floor plan, with the structure and technical services concentrated in a central core, at the top of which is the balcony. This arrangement partially eliminates the problem of future differential layout, without resorting to the use of piles.

183

KOZ Architectes (Plan 01)

House in Soulac-sur-Mer

This small wooden summerhouse is located 500 meters from the beach, on the dune of a small pine and oak forest. The architects were asked to design and implement the construction of the house, leaving the client to finish and fit it out himself. One of the design decisions that defined the house was the extensive use of wood, a material that the architects had previously used sparingly because of its relatively high cost. In this case they decided to take it further, without resorting to the use of a vocabulary of wooden construction and taking the overall budget into account. They quickly found the ideal material for the house: red cedar, a local wood that provides a link to the surroundings as well as a sense of scale and a particular kind of light. A living material for a living site, and an ideal "do-it-yourself" element for the client.

The architect's work then consisted of finding the way to implement the architectural elements of the design (lightness, discretion, luminosity, simplicity, varied and fluid relationship between the interior and the landscape) while respecting the requirements of the material (modularity, etc.) in order to optimize costs.

The house consists of a large platform that crosses the house, passing between two blocks containing the bedrooms. To the south it becomes a terrace shaded by oak trees, in the space between the blocks it becomes the living room, and to the north it is a lookout with views to the Cordouan lighthouse. This layout defines the house in its particular setting, between the microlandscape of the pine grove and the hugeness of the sea.

The southeast facade consists of blinds with slats made of wood, polycarbonate and cloth. This allows the house to change throughout the day, as the sunlight is filtered through the blinds.

In winter, the blinds can be raised in order to maximize the natural light in the interior.

Location: Soulac-sur-Mer, France

Photographs: J. M. Monthiers

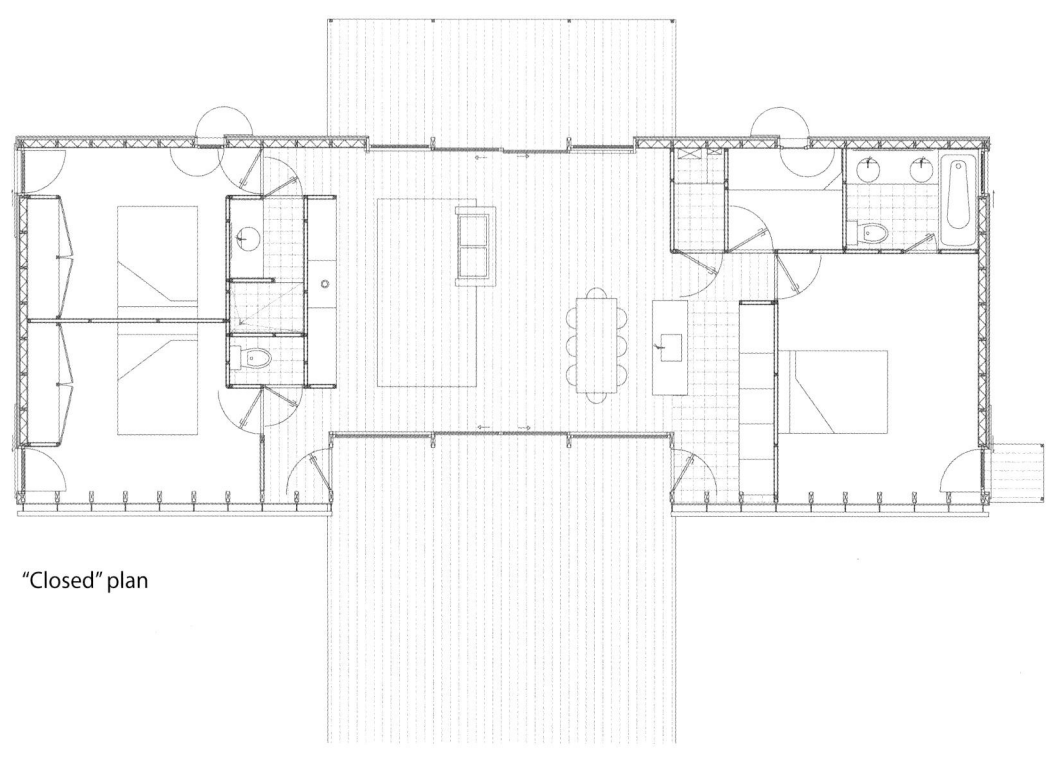

"Closed" plan

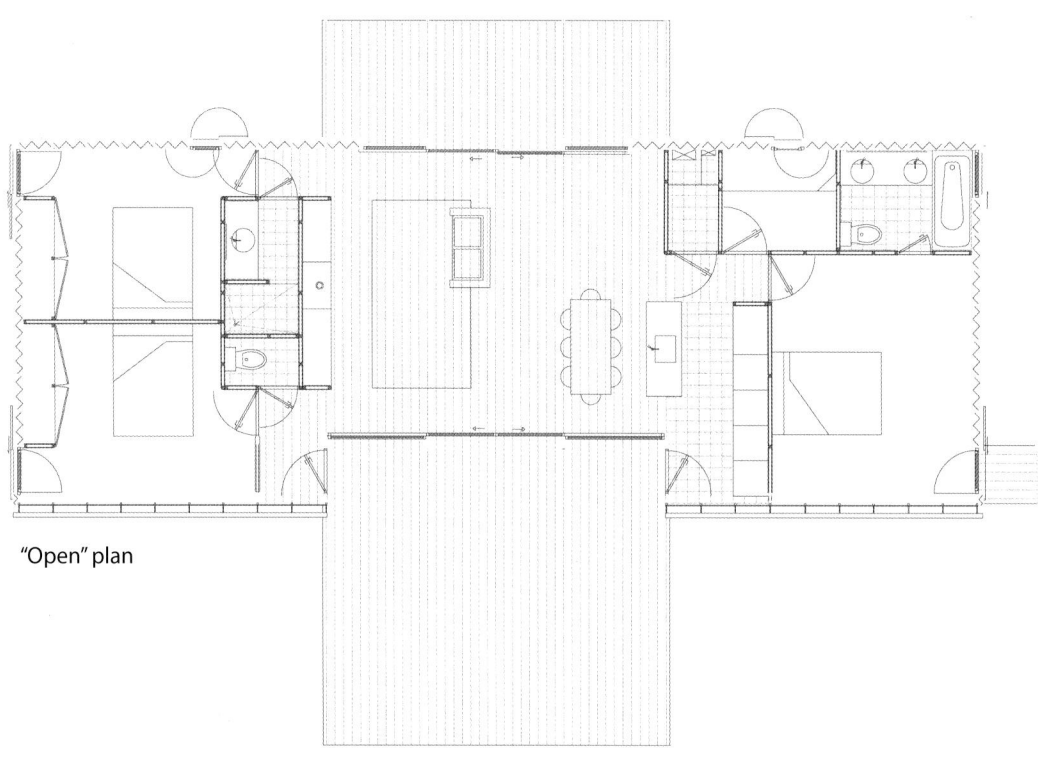

"Open" plan

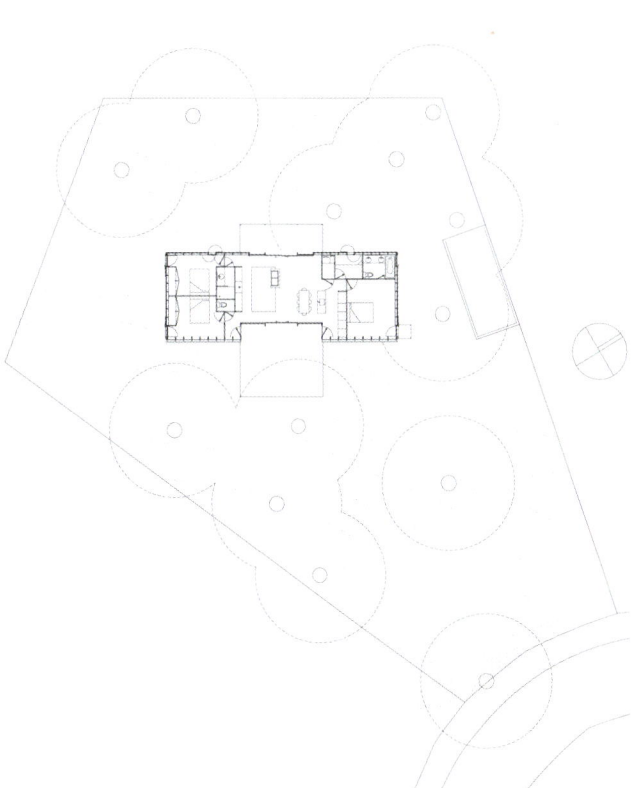

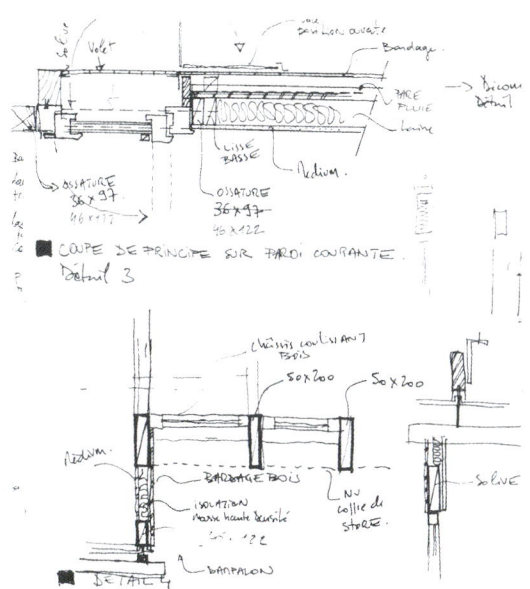

The use of wood from a local supplier was practical in terms of logistics, as it was "prefabricated" in the workshop and allowed the architects to manage the project remotely.

The building is raised off the building on slender colums, so that ther house seems to be suspended over the dune.

Takao Shiotsuka

Shigemi House

Various factors and considerations came into play when determining the final form that this house would take. Its unusual shape was developed for specific reasons. First was the wish to protect the façades, which are clad in wooden boards, from the rain. Another was to create the feeling of a spacious interior without actually increasing the ground space available. Additionally, continuity with the landscape was a goal. The access road slopes up toward the house, the embankment falls away on one side and rises on the other. So instead of standardized 90° angles, the architects instead opted for sloped façades.

The clients run a timber company and wished to fill the home, inside and out, with their company's product. Their original suggestion was to create wide eaves as a necessity for protecting the fine wood of the façades from the elements. Instead, the architects proposed tilting the perimeter walls outward, thus creating a unified shape that fulfilled the function of eaves. This exterior treatment has the additional advantage of broadening perspectives within the home as well. The total area of the ceiling is 130 sqm, while that of the floor space is 100 sqm.

Location:
Oita, Japan

Photographs:
Kaori Ichikawa

1. Entrance
2. Living room
3. Kitchen
4. Bedroom
5. Japanese tatami room
6. Storage
7. Bathroom
8. Lavatory

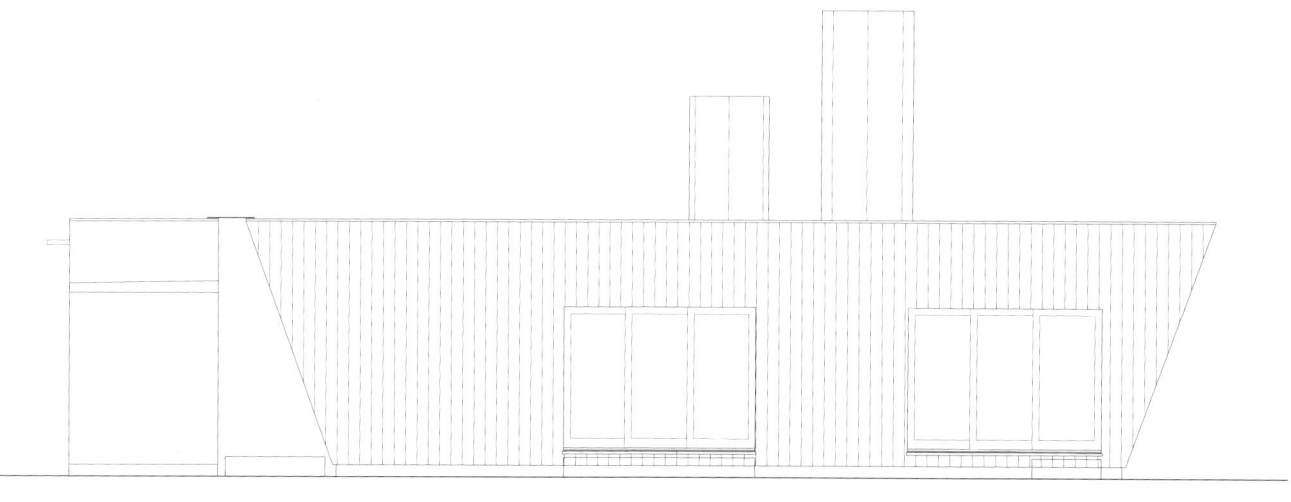
South elevation

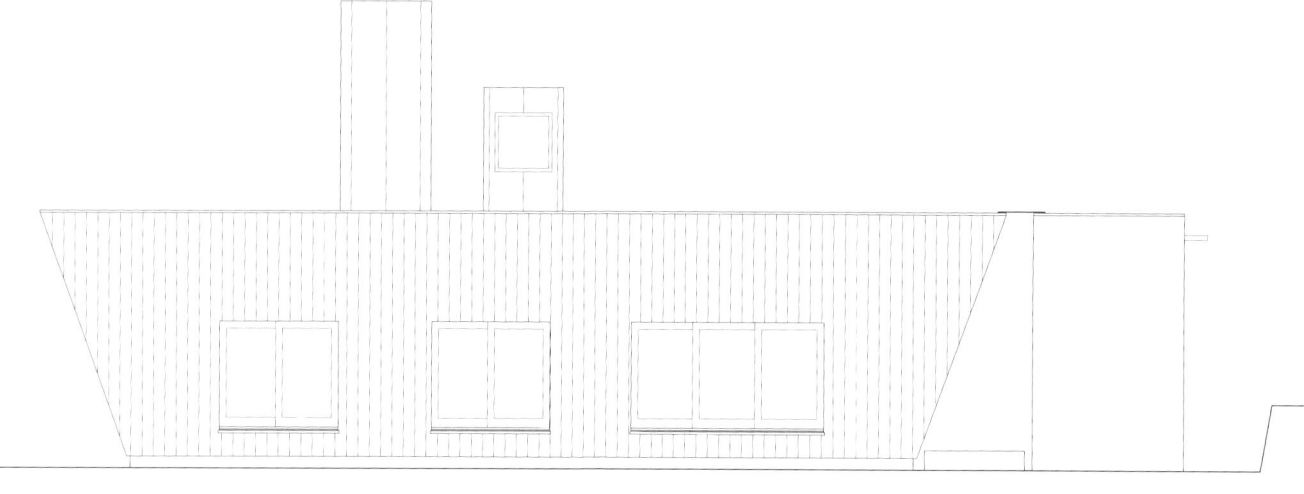
North elevation

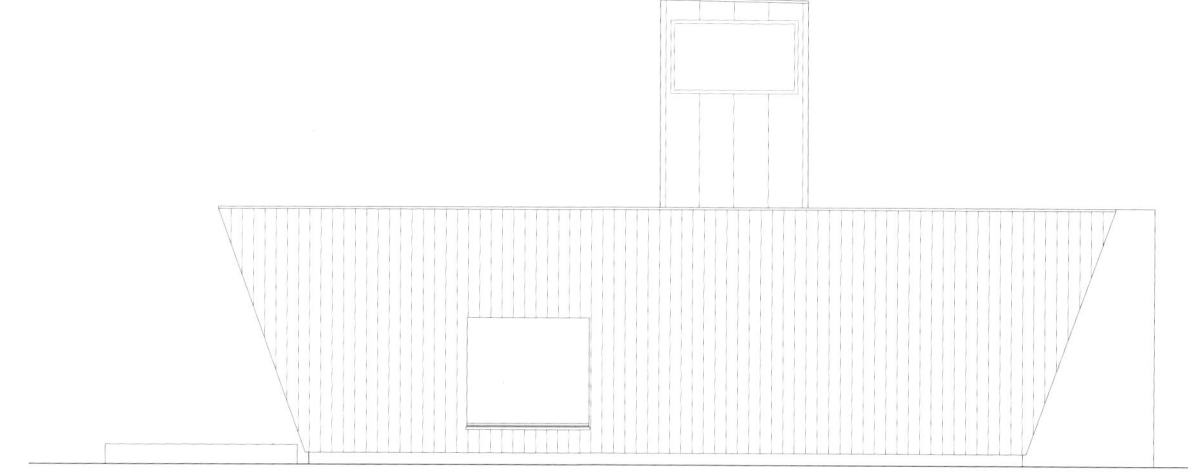
East elevation

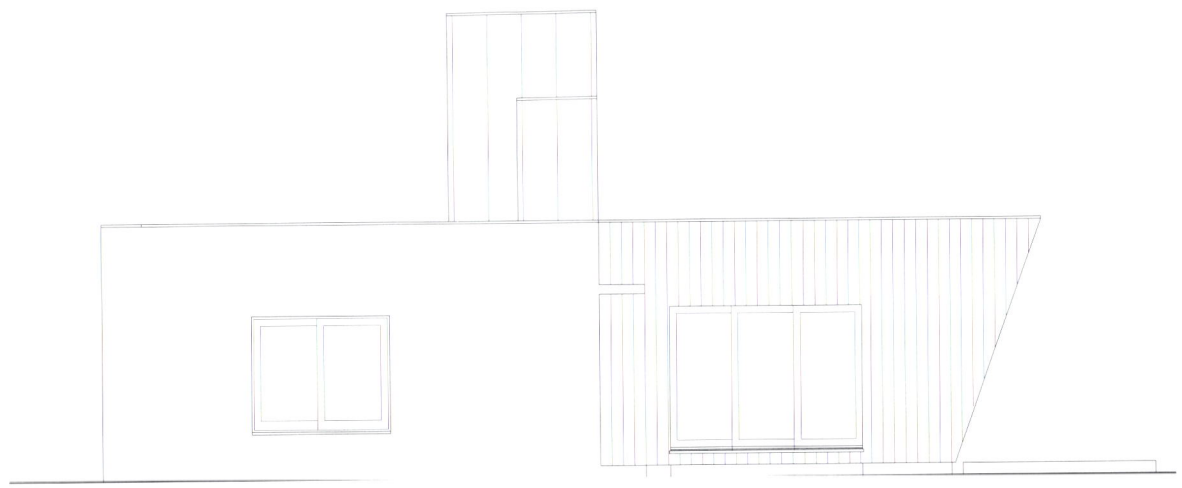

West elevation

Jarmund/Vigsnæs

Villa Flindt

Villa Flindt Vraalsen is a coastal property located on the peninsula of Nesodden, to the south of Oslo. The easiest route to this remote spot is via boat from the city center.

Set on a wild, rocky slope, the site's immediate natural surroundings combined with the far off views of Oslo (views which are particularly spectacular at night) make for an especially unique and aesthetically pleasing setting.

Furthermore, the conflicting desires to capture the greatest amount of sunlight (to the south) on the one hand and optimal views on the other (to the west as well as to the north) create an interesting tension in the project which has in fact become its guiding theme.

In the end, the living spaces were placed on the top floor, oriented to the north, where nighttime views are especially attractive. The kitchen and dining room, which open onto a spacious terrace, are also located here.

The lower floor houses the entrance and the bedrooms, which face more immediate views of the area's rugged nature. The concrete structure of the ground floor was poured in situ. It is clad in vertical wooden formwork, which precisely conforms to the natural granite rock contour of the side. All additional cladding is in Siberian larch wood.

Location:
Nesodden, Norway

Photographs:
Nils Petter Dale

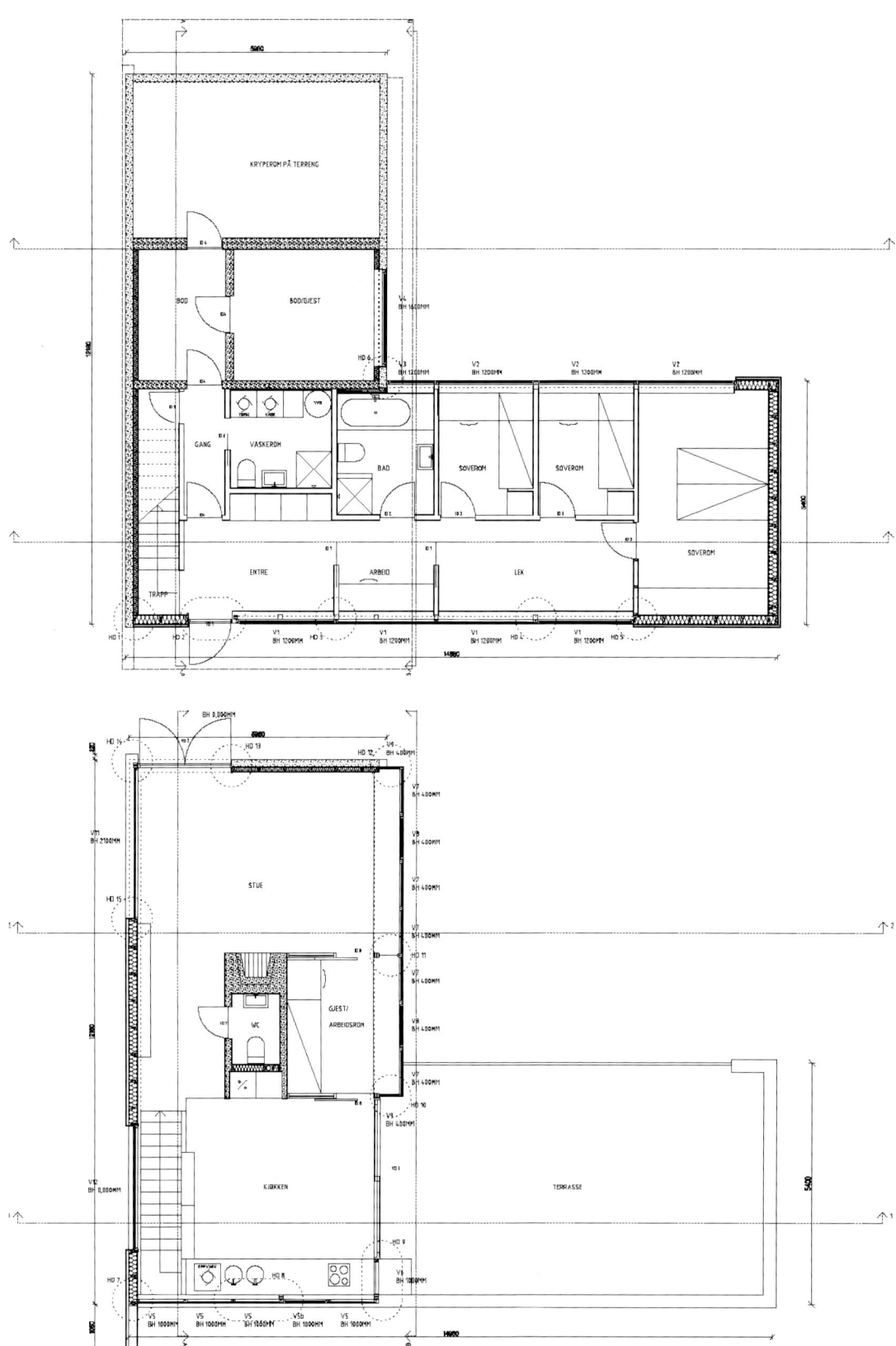

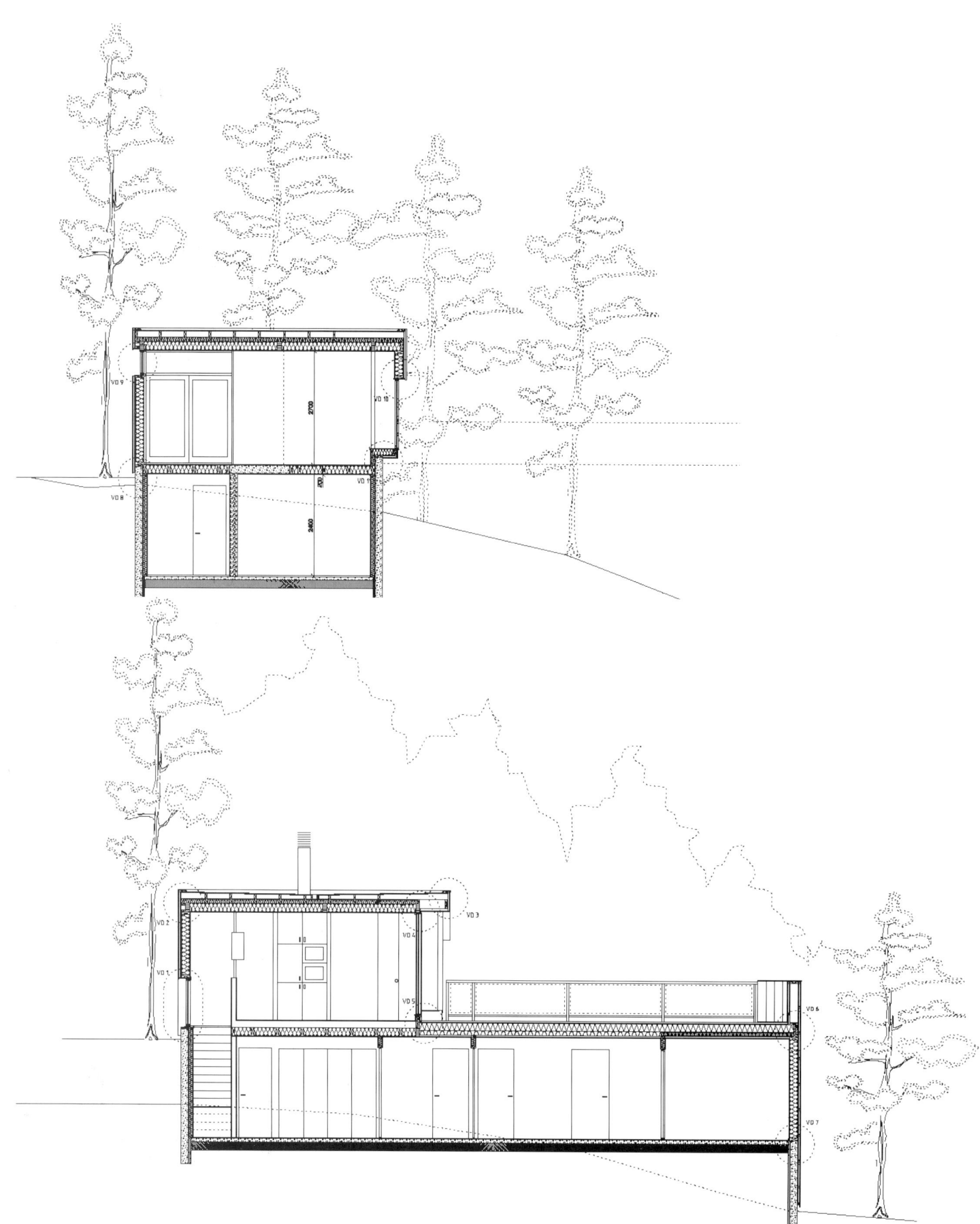

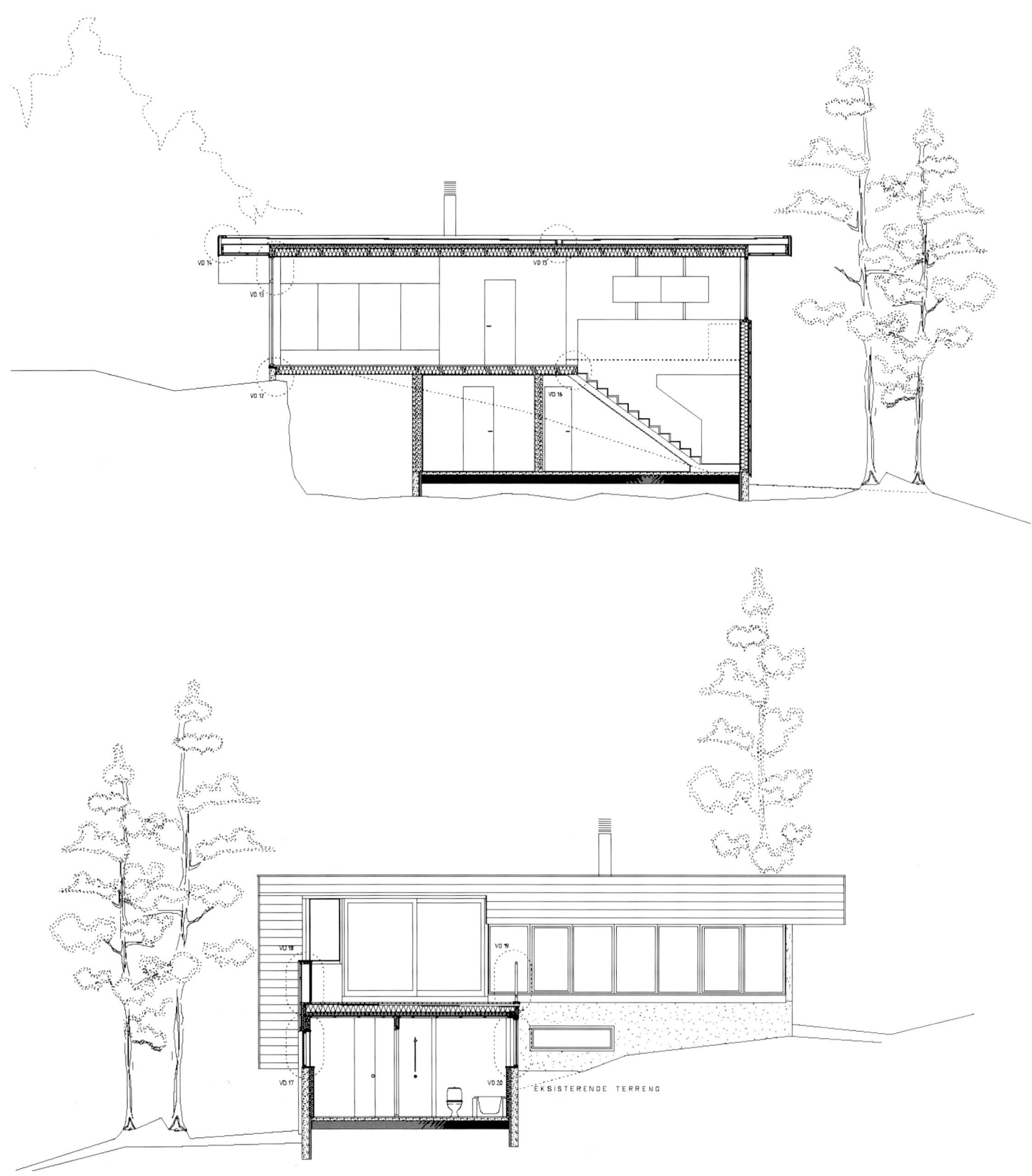

Hertl.Architekten

Steinwendtner House

The Steinwendtner House in Steyr-Münchholz was planned as a low-cost single-family house. The whole building is a timber construction, only the two containers in the garden that are used as a garage for bikes and also for garden tools are made of steel. In order to compensate for the smaller floor space the architect doubled the use of the aisle region as a passageway-room that is connected to the different rooms.

Once inside the house, one still can feel the volume of the whole building, a spaciousness that cannot be understood from the outside. The owners wanted a house protected from the views from the street. The solid façade of the south wall protects from view while the large glass wall of the first floor brings the southern daylight down in the living area. On the north side, the living area opens into the green of the nearby forest through a terrace that was cut out of the body of the building.

The analogy of the light-atmosphere to sacred places is throughout wanted.

Location:
Steyr-Munichholz, Austria

Photographs:
Paul Ott

Site plan

Layers

Exempted Box

Openings

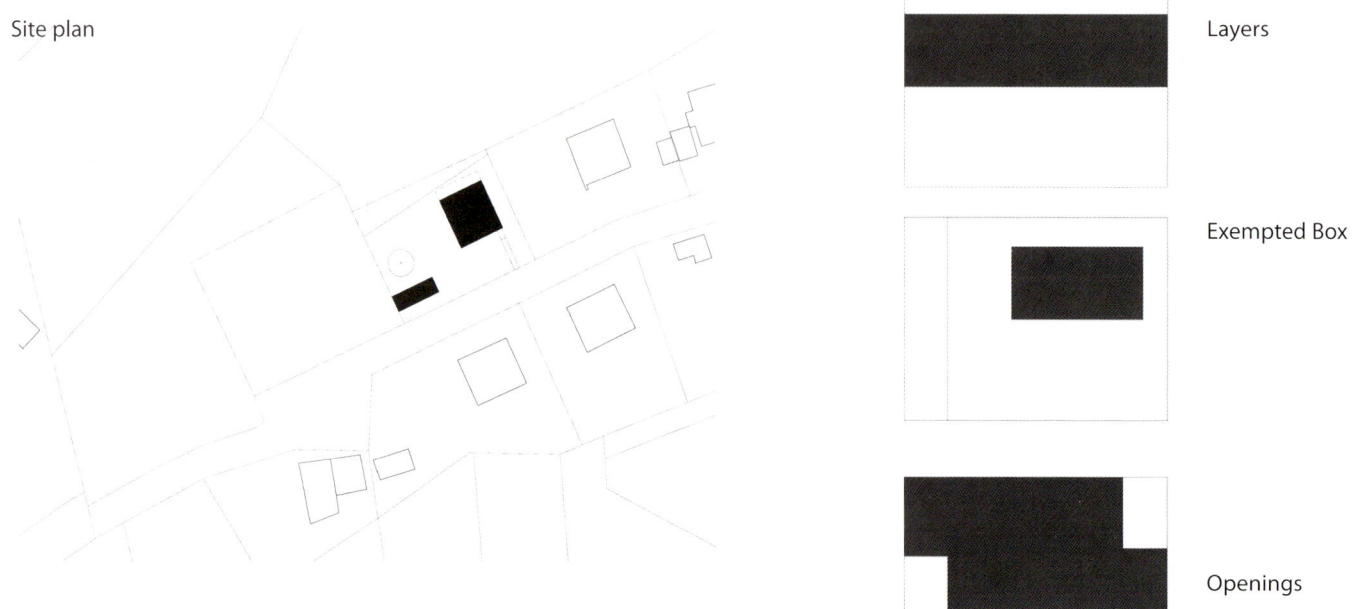

Ground floor plan

The Steinwendtner House in Steyr-Münchholz is a low-cost single-family house. The whole building is a timber construction.

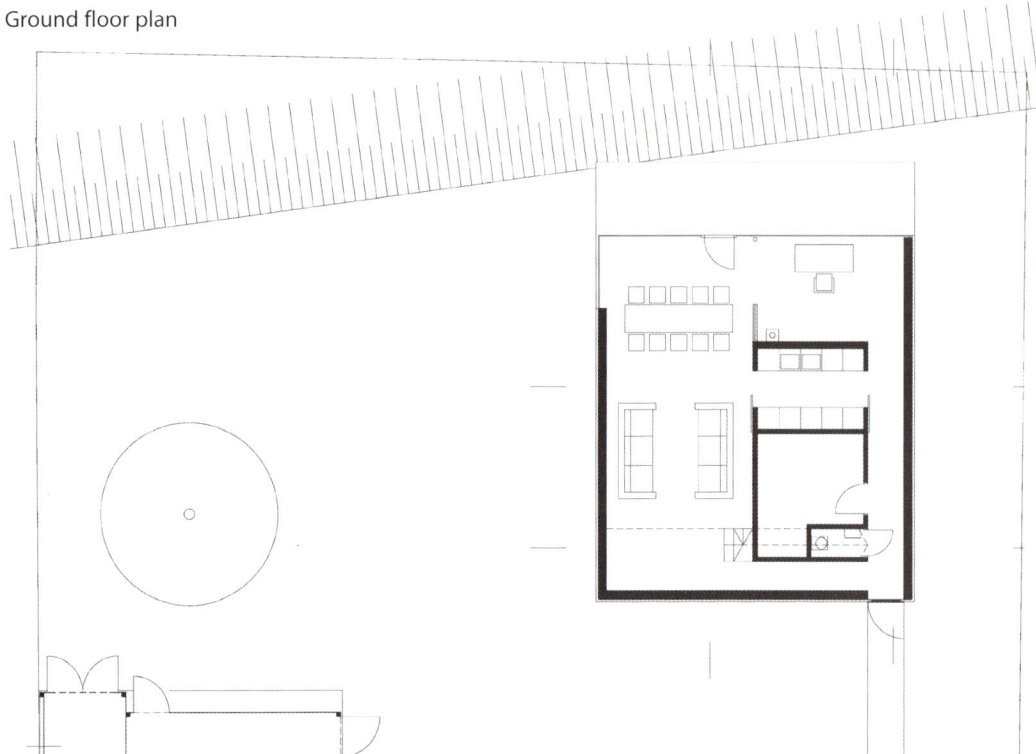

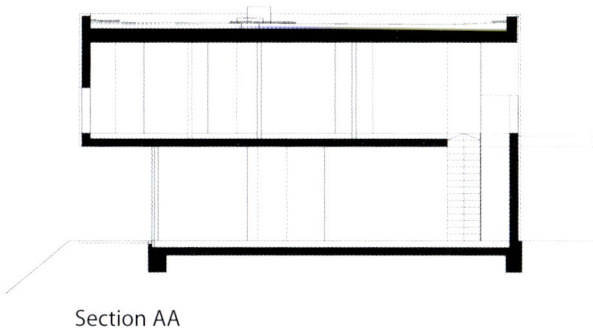

Section AA

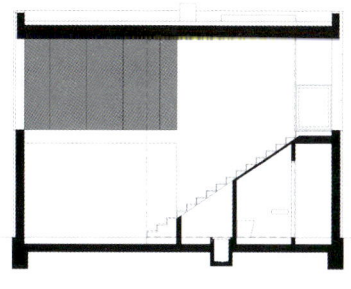

Section 11

Section BB

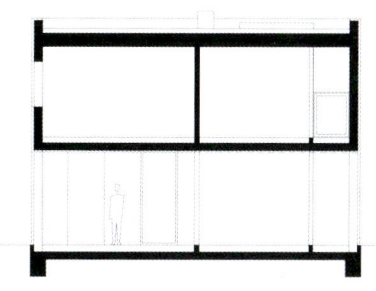

Section 22

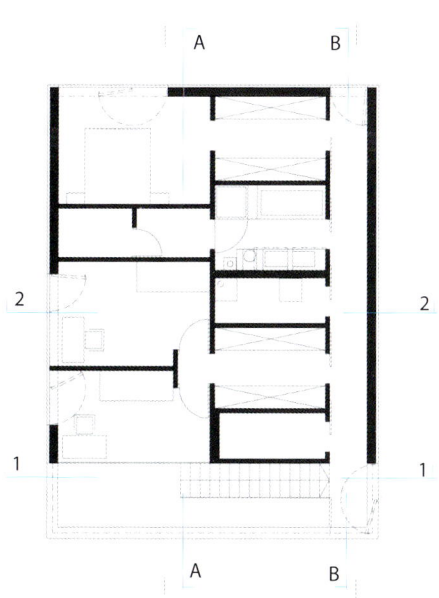

First floor plan

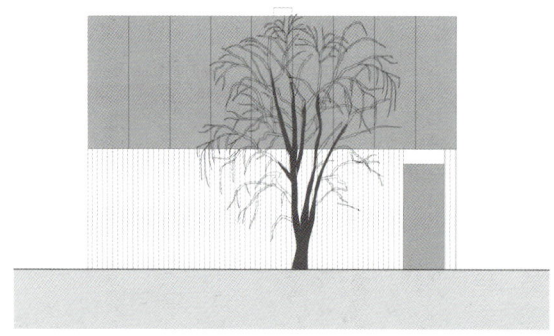

Southeast elevation

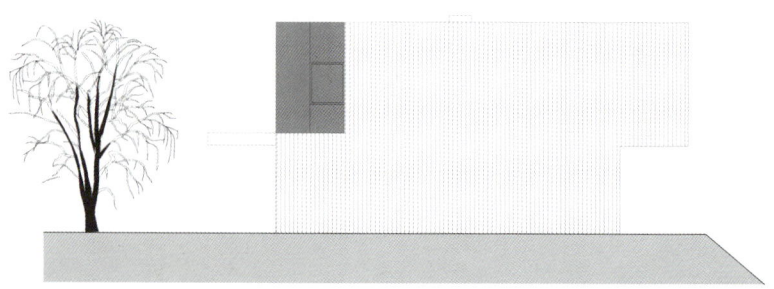

Northeast elevation

 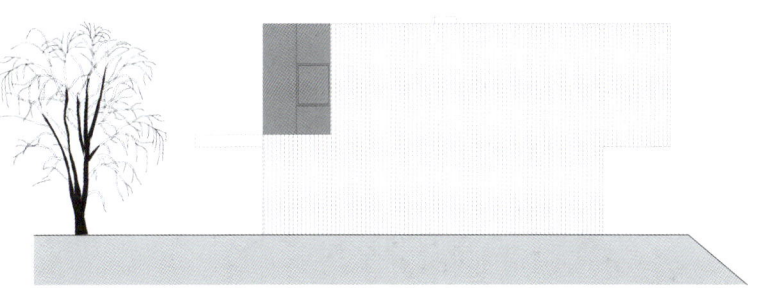

Southeast elevation

Northeast elevation

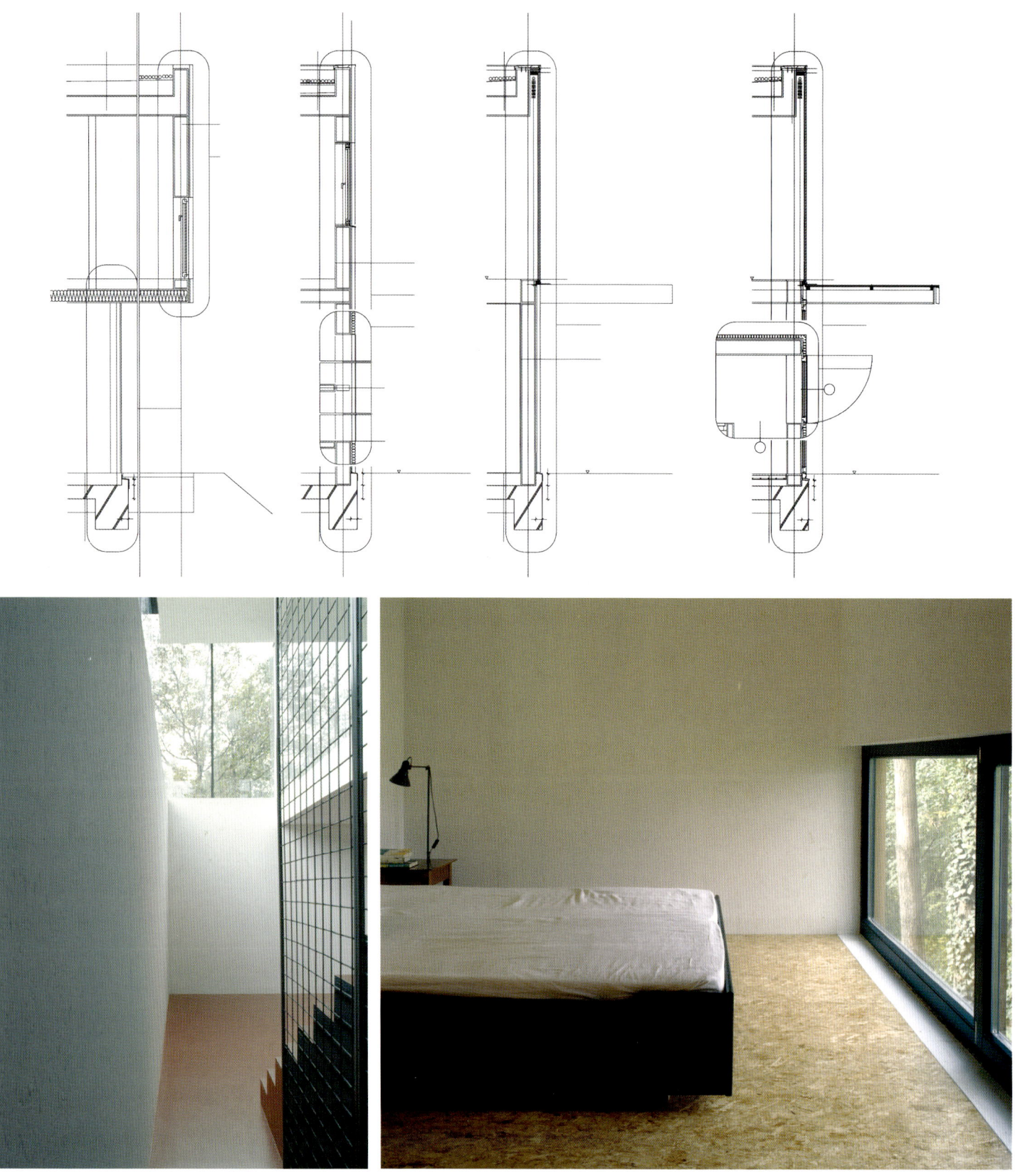

The living area receives southern light from the large glass wall of the first floor. On the ground floor, the south façade is closed to protect the living room from street views.

Strindberg Arkitekter AB

Villa Näckros

Situated on the east coast of Sweden, Villa Näckros is a world away from the traditional 'houseboats' of the past. Where floating homes have always been restricted in terms of both space and comfort, this one offers a spacious, contemporary living environment that combines all the luxuries of the modern day home with the spatial freedom and unrivalled views that only waterfront living can provide. One of Strindberg's key design solutions was to use repetition where possible. This worked to both simplify the construction process and help keep costs down. A spacious, light-filled home was achieved, in part, by dividing the space into a number of split-levels.

Encompassing 1916 square feet (178 square meters) of living space, set over three half levels, as well as a roof garden and terrace, the Villa's square shape evolved from the need to create a structure that would be as stable as possible. "We had to create something that would float, but designing a portable home was not the main objective in this case," explains Strindberg. "There was no need to assume the traditional shape of a boat."

The hull is constructed from reinforced concrete, which has been externally isolated to eliminate moisture on the inside. The weight of the concrete, combined with the shape of the hull, provides optimum stability. This method of construction has now been patented by the company. "Everything is glued together; there are no mechanical fastenings."

The main living area is characterized by large floor-to-ceiling windows, again overlooking the water. Oak flooring and neutral walls provide a blank canvas upon which to showcase the room's almost sculptural furnishings. Swathes of light also enable innovative pieces, such as the large white sculpture by Swedish sculptor Eva Hild and Olga Thorson's handmade ceramic 'Woman' lamp to create their own playful shadows across the floor. In the corner, a fireplace draws the eye upwards, emphasizing the room's double ceiling height. Carpeting has been used to subtly sub-divide and define the open plan living space, while Mats Theselius's Ambassad chairs, with their coppered steel frames upholstered in rivet prime leather, provide the perfect accompaniment to Mats Lindehoff's Kub tables.

Downstairs, the bedrooms have been designed with simplicity in mind. Built-in wardrobes create a clean line around the room's perimeter while the blind provides privacy without restricting the room's primary light source. A second of Olga Thorson's limited edition ceramic lamps - this time, 'Man' - provides an element of continuity whilst retaining its unique individuality.

Location:
Kalmar, Sweden
Photographs:
James Silverman

The red corrugated aluminum exterior and aluminum structure of the Villa provide a striking silhouette. Night façade lighting was designed by Andrew Gauld of gaulddesign.

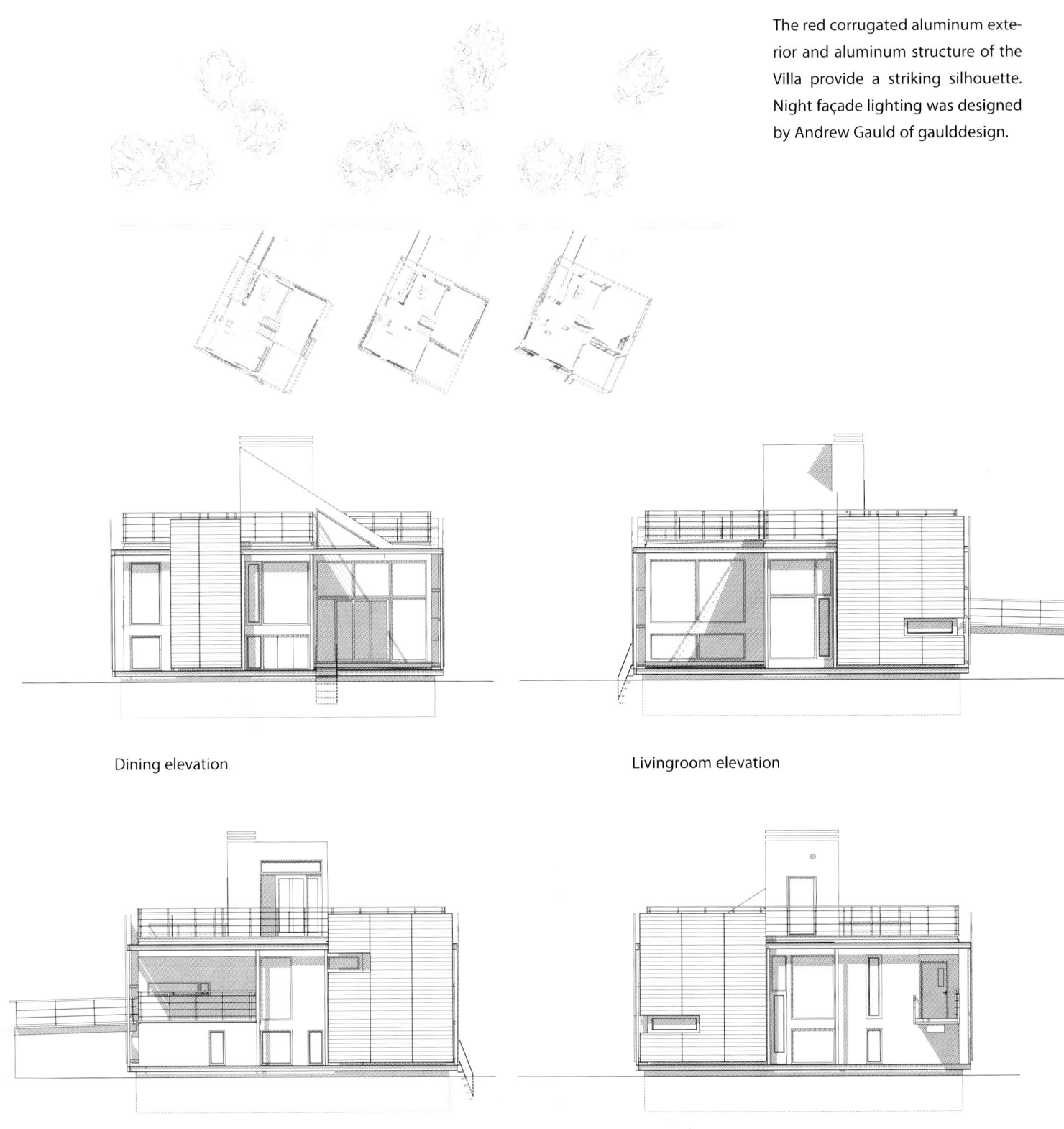

Dining elevation

Livingroom elevation

Entrance elevation

Kitchen elevation

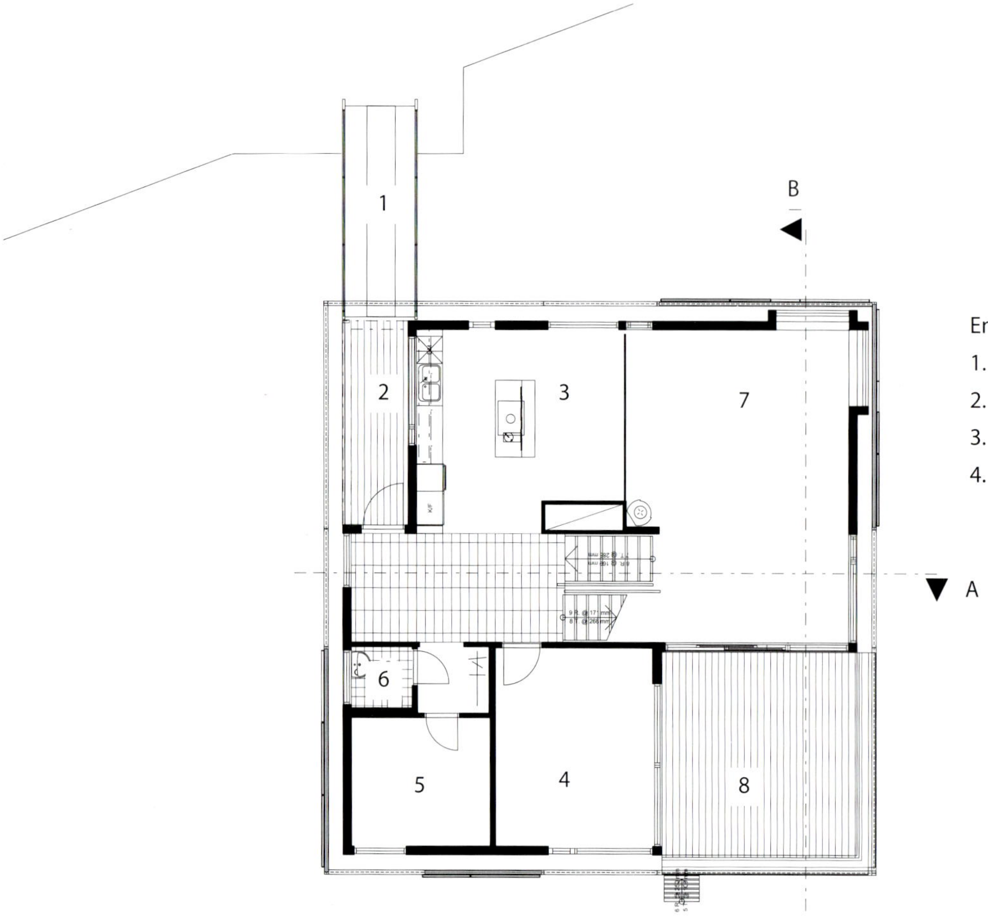

Entrance floor plan
1. Gangway
2. Entrance
3. Kitchen
4. Dining room
5. Study
6. WC
7. Living room
8. Terrace

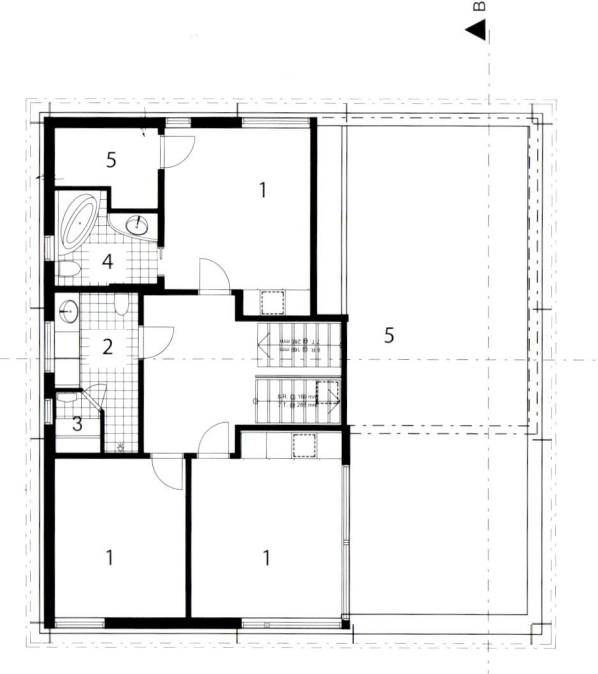

Ground floor plan
1. Bedroom
2. Bathroom / Laundry
3. Sauna
4. Bathroom
5. Mechanical equipment room
6. Store

Roof plan
1. Terrace
2. Kitchenette

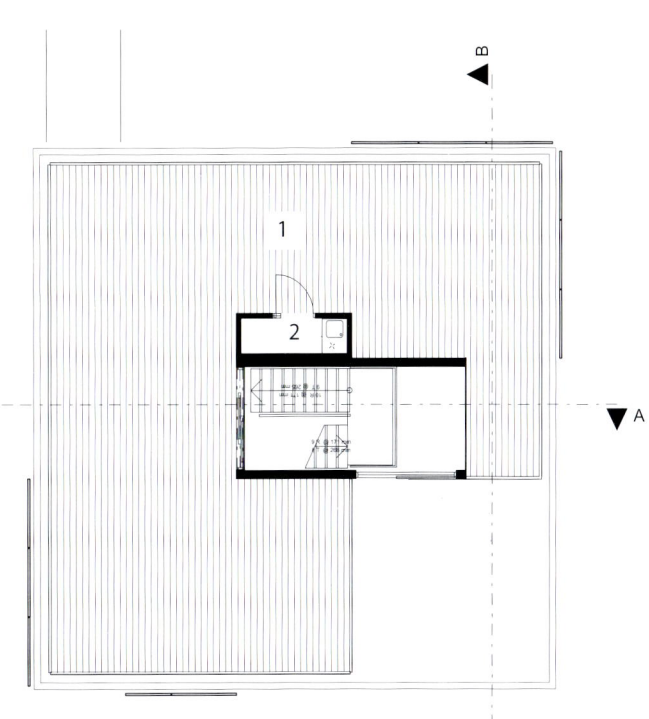

Section AA

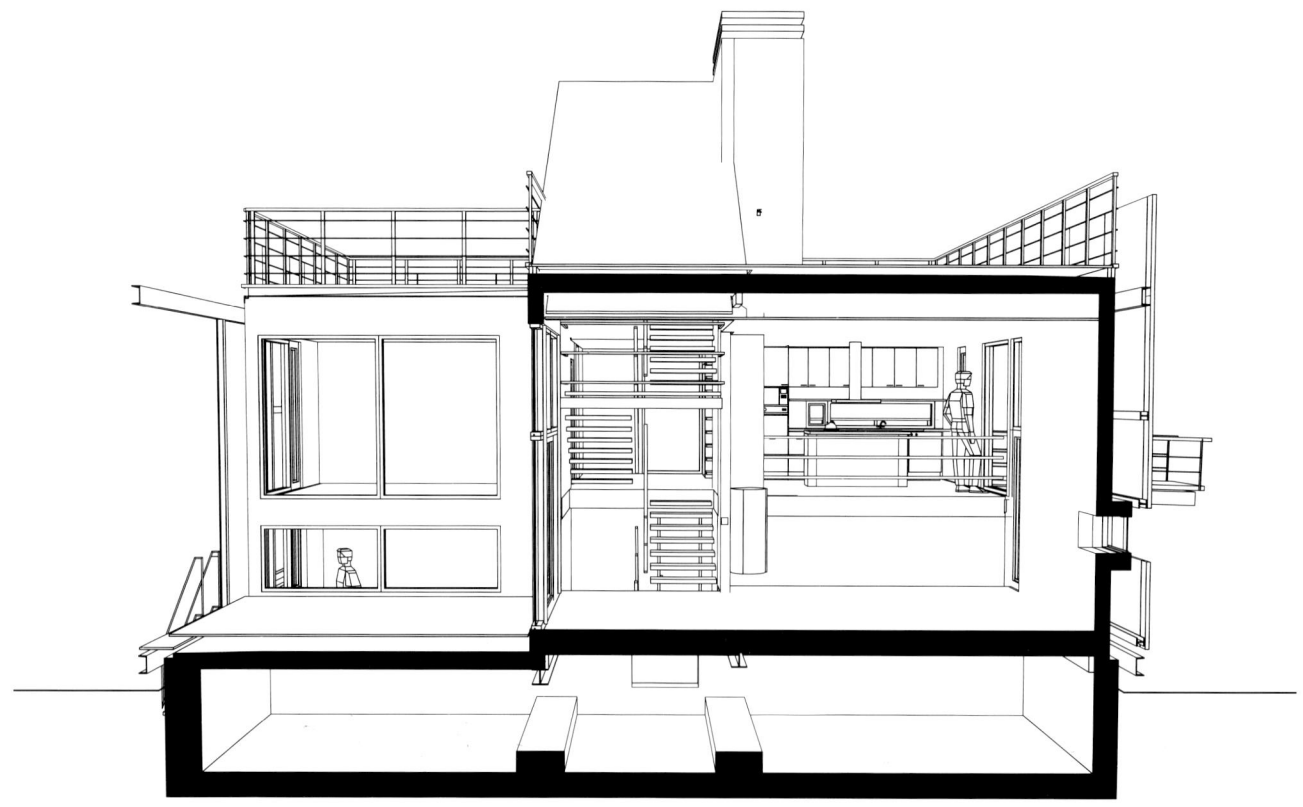

Section BB